UNFINISHED BUSINESS

STEPHANIE M. FREEMAN

Shadow Lilly Publications
York, Pennsylvania

Cover Designed by JL Woodson: www.woodsoncreative studio.com
Interior Designed by Lissa Woodson: www.Naleghnakai.com
Editors: Naleighna Kai and Kelsie Maxwell
Betas: Debra Mitchell, Brynn Weimer, April Bubb, Karen D. Bradley, and Kelsie Maxwell

UNFINISHED BUSINESS

For Dolores Ann Wilkes Freeman
"I kept my word."

For Tribe
Some families are birth made. Others are earth made.
You have my heart.
'If you want to go fast go alone. If you want to go far go
together.'
~African Proverb
I travel with my tribe.

We are only as good as the company we keep. Throughout the substantial edits and ultimate rebirth of this book, I had excellent company (and midwives). Thank you Naleighna Kai for all that you do today and every day. Special thanks to J.L Woodson for the awesome book cover! And to my Editors and Beta Readers Debra Mitchell, Brynn Weimer, Anita Roseboro- Wade, Karen D, Bradley, Kelsie Maxwell, and April Bubb. Thank you for your sharp eyes, attention to detail and your voracious appetites for reading!

We are only as good as the company we keep. Throughout the substantial edits and ultimate rebirth of this book, I had excellent company (and midwives). Thank you Naleighna Kai for all that you do today and every day. Special thanks to J.L Woodson for the awesome book cover! And to my Editors and Beta Readers Debra Mitchell, Brynn Weimer, Anita Roseboro- Wade, Karen D, Bradley, Kelsie Maxwell, and April Bubb. Thank you for your sharp eyes, attention to detail and your voracious appetites for reading!

To write is human, to edit is divine
- Stephen King

PROLOGUE

Blood never moved like water. Water was mindless yet persistent. Blood was deliberate, louder than an ocean, better than a scream.

Vincent was dead.

The fact that he was motionless on her bedroom floor was minutia. The dark patch of blood spread beneath the remains of his head in a gruesome cartoon bubble. Vincent's head was turned at an awkward angle, as if he were craning his neck to see where she'd gone. His gaze was vacant, but even on closed circuit television it still looked like he was staring at her, blaming her.

Mamma mustn't know.

It had been Monet's deal breaker. Vincent was *her* secret. Having one aspect of her life that Mamma didn't know about made her feel mature, like she was capable of being anything other than who she was. Surely, they'd understand; someone had to understand. Monet needed to get out from under the shadow.

Imagine a demon raising a child.

Admiration dripped from the corners of his smile whenever he spoke. Vincent always formed the words slowly so that Monet Garrett could read his lips. Most hearing people mumbled or forgot to face her. Cleaning her with a warm, wet washcloth after making love was his idea of 'white glove service'. Dressing Monet in his pajama top made it romantic. But then the laser light pierced the darkness and Vincent jerked and fell on top of her. Extricating herself from the organic prison of his dead weight was nearly impossible. By the time she did, the lights flickered, alerting her that someone was at the front door. The panic room was closer.

Mamma has her secrets, and I have mine.

Monet turned her face into her shoulder and let the tears come. She wiped at the tears and brain matter on her face with her sleeve and licked her lips. The coppery taste she expected wasn't there. Cherry flavored corn syrup filled her mouth along with bits of fruit leather.

It didn't register at first what she was seeing. The cartoon bubble of blood was still there on the carpet, but Vincent wasn't. He was the only one that knew the code to open the door.

Monet had stood up when she saw the yellow light from the touch lamp on her bedside table pour through the crack in her panic room doorway. Unspent shell casings rolled across the floor like roaches scurrying from the light.

She palmed the butt of the 15-round magazine into the Glock 19 and took in steadying breath as her mother's, Alana Symone, words filled her head.

Center of mass for everything, Monet. You can't afford anything else.

The flash from the muzzle frightened and exhilarated her, but something was wrong. Vincent was alive and still coming toward her.

The muscles in her arm went limp as she spilled back to the floor and stared at the gun. Vincent walked over and stooped down. He tried to smooth a hand over her hair, and she knocked it away. Vincent snatched up the gun and backhanded her into the wall.

Monet spat at the taste of rust that filled her mouth. She could see his mouth moving over his red-stained teeth. There was no need for him to sign. He spoke slowly, the way he always did.

"You were worth every penny."

Vincent turned to say something over his shoulder, and Monet drove the switchblade she had hidden in her pajama pocket into his arm and twisted it into his shoulder. He turned around and punched her, making her see brilliant flecks of light as her head thumped against the wall once more.

CHAPTER 1

Alana wasn't there.

Cass rolled over onto his back and reached across the bed. Judging from the lack of her body heat in the sheets Alana hadn't been there for a while. He sat up and pulled on a pair of grey sweatpants to go with the black tank top and boxers that clung to his massive muscular frame.

He peered into his son Gabriel's room. Cass's cat, Jasper, died years ago. The old Egyptian Mau had been replaced by a retired police dog named Whiskey. The dog lifted its head and sniffed the air in Cass's direction before settling down once more.

The chill in the air, the stillness of the house, made the hair on the back of Cass's neck stand up. The same eerie feeling had descended on him earlier that evening when Alana excused herself from the table.

Her gaze seemed to be riveted to the window at the front of Delia's, an Italian Bistro near the Inner Harbor. People passed by with little, or no, notice of what was going on inside. When Alana didn't return to the table, Cass got up and went to look for her. Alana was outside handing a cup of soup and a business card to a teenage girl.

The whole scene was nothing new. Alana always seemed to know when a girl was fresh off the bus from nowhere. But something about the exchange bothered him. The girl was arguing with Alana. The girl looked up in the middle of whatever she was saying, saw him, and took off.

Cass shook off the memory until they arrived back at Mark and Myra's, and Alana disappeared from the table where Myra had put out birthday cake and coffee. Again, Cass excused himself and went searching for his wife. He found her on the front porch crouching down as she stared out at the street.

The fact that it was February and there was snow on the ground barely seemed to faze Alana. Her biracial features took on a pale shade of blue in the winter moonlight.

Myra, Cass' best friend Mark's wife, had insisted—as she had since the day Alana walked out of prison and straight into Cass's arms— that February twelfth was Alana's birthday and as such they would celebrate. Alana quietly accepted the date and the occasion with her usual bemused look. Tonight, the distraction in her face made Cass reach for her more than once.

At home, Cass stood in the doorway and watched as Alana carefully put Gabriel to bed. He had gone down to check the doors one last time, when he heard the soft strains of music emanating from their bedroom.

He followed the jazzy version of My Funny Valentine to find Alana staring out their bedroom window. Cass drew her into an embrace, and they danced. As he drew her closer, he breathed her in and turned his face down against her ear.

"Babe what's wrong?"

Alana simply turned and nudged a kiss out of him. The taste of her, the smell of her, was always enough to make him forget the world.

Cass shook off the memory and made his way downstairs. He glanced over the banister into the small breakfast nook to find the kitchenette set he'd made for her apartment years ago silently waiting for her to return with one of the many books she had housed in her massive library in their den. He took the last four steps in twos as his heart began to pound against his ribs.

He palmed the light switch on, bathing their living room in a soft, warm yellow. Alana's rocking chair sat silent, with one of her many shawls spilling over the back. More of her books sat neatly on the coffee table, waiting for her. Cass was about to draw in a breath to yell her name when he saw her silhouette against the moonlight pouring through their patio door.

The kitchen was dark, yet the moonlight spilled in, casting everything around her in a silvery blue haze. The sheet she wore spilled from one shoulder, exposing her back. The scars he saw there still made him fill up from time to time. Cass had kissed every one of them and tried to love away the ones inside Alana, but he knew on some level that there was no salve to erase the memories.

One look at the burn scars on his own hands was enough to remind him. Apart, he and Alana were walking wounds. Together, they were living proof that, like many things in life, some nightmares never faded. Some were meant to be remembered and endured. Cass opened the door and stood there. The ice in the air made his eyes water and his nose burn.

"When you first came home, I'd find you outside like this. Crouching down as if you were hunkering down for a war. "Scanning the back yard, he ventured another look at her before settling against the doorframe. "Haven't seen you do that in years…. until tonight at Mark and Myra's."

"You would ask me what was wrong." Her voice sounded hollow against the blue black of night.

"You would say 'nothing' then you'd come back to bed and make love to me and…" Cass moved closer, almost afraid to touch her.

"You thought I was lying." In one fluid motion she rose and turned to face him. Alana's green witch-like gaze shifted slowly over his features.

After all those years, it still hurt to look at her full on. The hard, hunted look was gone, but her haunting, unconventional beauty remained. The ancient, hard-won wisdom he saw there was tempered by a profound love that still shook him to his core.

"Never thought you were lying. I just felt like...you were keeping something. Withholding some part of yourself from me."

"You know everything that's worth knowing about me." She shrugged, crowding into his space.

"But if you thought it would keep me or the children out of harm's way... I know the types of promises you keep... the cost?" He swallowed trying to ignore the dread winding its way through his blood. "Baby, please, tell me what's wrong. Let me make it better. At least let me try."

"Shh. I'm just waiting." Her voice, barely more than a whisper, bathed his bare skin in kisses as she moved closer.

"For what, honey?" He slipped an arm around her waist and recoiled at the stone-cold feel of her. "Jesus Christ, Alana, you're like ice." Cass reached for the sheet to pull it up onto her shoulders and just as he brought Alana to his chest, her legs gave out.

CHAPTER 2

Nicholas Levine stared at the computer monitor. Every time he looked up from his current case files, the picture of Alana Symone stared back at him. Her eyes seemed to be riveted to him, telling him nothing while demanding everything. It wasn't even his case anymore. It wasn't even a cold case. Things had died down years ago. Unless someone was looking right at her file, no one knew there was such a thing as Alana Symone. She could never be mistaken for a former cheerleader trying to relive her youth through her daughter.

Alana was her mugshot: ageless... ethereal... deadly. She was the only woman he knew that wasn't even trying, yet her mugshot was much like she was: artwork. She wasn't pretty. Babies and small children were pretty. Alana wasn't made up to look like anything important, but there was something below her surface. It shifted behind her emerald-colored eyes and made her seem a little less than human, too much like royalty.

She had the type of frail beauty that made men want to take care of her, want to know what her kisses taste like. Then there was the other side of her: a cunning side, a ruthless side that gave her a savage beauty. With a cryptic smile he knew that she was far more dangerous than anything or anyone he had ever encountered in his entire career.

Siren... Mermaid... Alana embodied the mythical creatures he'd read about as a boy. When he'd first laid eyes on her years ago, as she crouched down on the floor in the corner of the interrogation room, Levine had wondered if Alana had the same gifts those creatures possessed.

Could she lure men to their deaths? He glanced up into her emerald eyes once more.

Of course, she could.

Lots of men that had crowded around her were no longer among the living. Most, if not all, were glad to go. Only one remained, one that was still willing to kill or be killed for her. Levine shook his head and looked away from the picture.

Levine had inherited the Symone case from his old partner, Patrick Cohn, and even he didn't talk about it. All Cohn would say was, "You had to be there to believe it."

Patrick Cohn was a methodical and deliberate FBI Agent that only pulled his gun twice in the line of duty. The man everyone called Teacher looked more like a librarian or a college professor and was well suited for either job with his freakish knowledge about obscure subjects.

Teacher was the only man Levine knew that never raced into action when a call came in. Instead, he continued to work quietly, gathering up whatever files he'd been working on, as if he were waiting for a silent alarm to go off in his head. Only then would Teacher shrug into his nondescript brown coat and pick up his car keys.

Then there was the case of Alana Symone.

Levine heard the whispers but none of them made sense. He was new to the agency and not privy to 'The Case' as everyone called it at the time. The one time Levine broached the subject with Teacher, the man merely looked at him. The deadness in his eyes said it all. Years later, as Teacher waited, in hospice, for the prostate cancer to finish him, he pointed with a pale liver-spotted hand to the footlocker sitting in the corner of the room.

Even then, what he said made little sense.

"She has lived in denied territory for so long, I rather think it's home for her. She can exist and even be happy where she is. Yes, I think she is happy."

Levine was fresh from a contract working for the Department of Defense. He understood the term 'denied territory' as an area under enemy or unfriendly control in which friendly forces cannot expect to operate successfully within existing operational constraints and force capabilities.

Levine sighed and looked up into that silent green gaze. His partner, Arence "AJ" Fischer, flopped down in his chair across from Levine and put his feet up on the desk. AJ stretched and rubbed at a new injury to his shoulder.

"Looks like you've been in the batting cages, AJ." Levine watched the man settle back in his chair and smile.

AJ leaned over and glanced at Levine's monitor. "You still haven't made the call, have you? There's no sign of her anywhere."

Levine looked over at his monitor and shuffled the papers back into the file.

"She's in New Serenity, Maryland, right?" AJ grabbed the landline receiver and wedged it between his shoulder and his ear.

Levine chuckled and sat back. "You sure you want to poke that particular pair of bears? You've met Cassiel and Alana Garrett. They are the only people I know that have '*Don't fuck with me.*' written all over them."

AJ hung up the phone and settled back in his chair. "You make her seem like she's untouchable. Hell, what am I saying? She is. She's got the golden parachute to end all golden parachutes. The only one the attorney general handed down ironclad. I mean, nobody could touch it. One year in federal for all the shit she pulled. She'll play nice if she knows what's good for her."

"Not every prison has walls you know." Levine swallowed at the acid rising in the back of his throat.

"Now you sound just like the old man. So what if she refused witness protection?"

Levine chuckled as he fished in the drawer for the bottle of acid reducer medication. "Patrick Cohn did have a way."

"Well, Teacher is long gone. Now you're the Dali Lama of this place. Everybody knows they're fixing up your office upstairs. Just make the call."

Levine leaned over and turned off his flat screen monitor. "You don't deliver this kind of news over the phone. No parent ever could."

CHAPTER 3

When he got her back in bed, he stripped out of his night clothes and covered her with his body. Cass gritted his teeth against the cold as he wrapped his arms and legs around her and drew her even closer.

He tried not to think of it, but the memories were there. Cass could still feel her slam into him as the bullets tore through her to get to him. As her blood spilled into his chest and spread on the floor beneath him, this was how she felt.

She was cold, lifeless. She'd smiled so cryptically. "I won," she'd said as if dying were some exotic prize. Back then it seemed to be the only prize she wanted. Back then it was the only gift she thought she could give him.

The years flew by, and before he knew it he was making and selling his furniture and taking an occasional assignment as a security consultant for the government. Alana was the manager of her own center for runaways. Life had been good. Cass thought of his son and their daughter away at college. Life had been more than good.

When the stale blueness of morning crept through the curtains and she began to warm beneath him, only then did he allow himself to drift off. Cass instantly came awake when he felt her smooth her hand over his back. Alana parted her thighs to welcome him closer. He gently but firmly slipped his knee between them.

He looked down into the fathoms of her green gaze before he gave her a long, languid kiss. "Not until you explain what you meant before you passed out last night."

Alana ran her hand gently over the scar on his cheek as an ancient sadness gathered in the corners on her eyes. She blinked, and the sadness was gone. She turned her head towards the sounds of their son singing to himself in the bathroom down the hall. "I'll go make breakfast."

Cass captured her cheek against the warm wall of his hand and made her look at him. "Our son knows how to fix a bowl of cereal. Stay here. When he's gone, we talk."

Alana moved to protest, and Cass moved his knee and drove himself deep within her. She writhed beneath him as he ground his hips into hers. He continued to pace his rhythmic strokes until he heard her breathing change. Just when he was sure he was about to spill his measure into her, and her own orgasm was close, he withdrew and slipped his knee between her thighs once more. Alana arched her back as she winced in pain.

"What... Cassiel don't... please..."

The sound of her plea was almost his undoing. Cass flattened himself against her for the briefest moment, summoned all his strength and looked at her once more. "Not until you tell me what's wrong."

Cass nipped at her mouth again before he climbed over her and moved to their bathroom. Alana started to follow. "Stay there. I mean it," he called over his shoulder. "When you're ready to talk, come find me."

CHAPTER 4

Cass leaned against the kitchen counter drinking a cup of coffee as his son Gabriel finish his breakfast.

"Mom was up again last night, wasn't she?" Cass sat his cup aside and joined his son at the table. "Yeah, bud, she was." He started putting Gabriel's books in his navy-blue backpack.

"She okay?" Gabriel's green gaze drifted slowly to Cass's face as he spooned in another mouthful of cereal. The milk dribbled down his chin.

Cass passed him a napkin. "Why do you ask?"

"It's just sometimes she gets this look on her face. I don't know, like she's scared she's going to forget where she put me. Like last night at Aunt Lydia's."

"What do you mean?"

"Mom checked the window to make sure it was locked. When we got here, she did the same thing. She even went into Mo's room, carried me in there like she didn't trust the house."

"I check the locks too," Cass offered, but he knew what his son was saying. "Does it bother you that she's so careful with you?" Cass avoided the frown on his son's face.

"We matter to Mom. I think it makes her sleep better when we're okay. When I was little, before you two left the agency, she would sleep on the floor next to my bed."

"Son, I slept on the floor by Monet's bed while your Mom was in prison. Your sister was so small back then, little more than a baby herself. I woke up to her asleep on my back more than once. I'd put her back in bed, then I'd wake up in the morning and there she was again asleep on my back."

Gabriel bit down on his lip and mulled for a bit then shook his head. "When Mo was here, we would camp out in your room watching movies. We would have peanut butter cookies and green tea. I'd wake up later and there was Mom, looking out the window."

"You want her to stop tucking you in?"

"She shouldn't be carrying me around anymore. I'm a big guy you know." Gabe nodded." What if I hurt her? She holds me like she's afraid she's gonna lose me. You saw what happened when the bus driver dropped me off on the wrong corner."

Cass shuddered at the memory. He'd watched in horror as she stepped into its path, forcing the woman driving to stomp on the breaks so hard that the tires screeched. Alana clawed the door open and boarded the bus.

She had slammed the door shut before Cass could climb aboard to stop her. She'd never said what she told the woman. The very next day the bus had a new driver, and Alana picked Gabriel up from school from then on.

"You want me to talk to her," Cass asked as he zipped the backpack, sat it aside and tucked a couple of napkins in his matching lunchbox.

"I just want to make her feel safe, Dad; as safe as she makes me feel." Gabe frowned and a runnel of milk spilled over his chin.

Cass dabbed at the milk with another napkin and smiled. "Hey, that's my job when you're at school. You wanna stay here today? Maybe you can help me in the shop?"

Gabe shook his head and stuck another spoonful of colorful marshmallows and cereal bits into his mouth. "Test day. Mom gets mad when I miss a test." He chewed thoughtfully and swallowed.

Just then they both heard the air brakes whine as the bus pulled to a stop outside. Gabe ran over and hugged his father. Cass helped him into his coat and put his backpack on him.

As an afterthought, Cass hugged him again and pressed a kiss to the top of his son's head.

"You gonna show me how to put the grippers on my skateboard?" Gabriel squirmed in his arms so that he could look up at his father.

"Hey, that was supposed to be your birthday gift, nosy." Cass pinched his son's nose gently.

"I know, but I saw it sitting in the vise earlier when I went to see if the stain was dry on the porch swing we're working on for Mom." Gabe flashed him a smile that reminded Cass that the tooth fairy needed to tuck a dollar or two under his pillow.

"Sure, Gabe. I'll pick you up after school. You can pick out the grippers you want."

"Mom always comes to get me. She said I need a new coat, but I like this one fine. Maybe we can get her to make some spaghetti tonight." As an afterthought, Gabriel reached up and tapped his father on the forehead.

"Hey, what are you up to?" He grabbed his son's hand and rubbed some warmth into it before he tugged a glove onto Gabriel's hand.

"Mom does that to me a lot, especially on test days. She taps me on the forehead and keeps saying. *You need to be smarter than me.*' How is that even possible? You built the bookcases for her library. Her library could *eat* the one at my school, Dad."

Cass chuckled as Gabriel tugged his hat down over his shock of red curly hair.

Cass watched as his son boarded the bus, knowing that Alana was doing the same thing from an upstairs window. Even if the driver was standing right at the front window looking in, Cass knew the old guy would never see her.

CHAPTER 5

The soft scent of her juniper berry bath soap found him before her hand came to rest between his shoulders. Cass took in a deep, shuddery breath and followed her to the kitchen. His old, grey Quantico sweatshirt spilled from her bare left shoulder.

Alana's hips swayed gently as she moved around the table and snagged his mug. She cradled the mug in both hands as she took a sip. She glanced over her shoulder and frowned before turning back to the coffee maker. He fingered her damp, careless ponytail before he took his chair again.

Cass watched as she made herself a cup of coffee and topped off his mug. When she slipped into their son's chair, Cass extended both of his hands toward her. He marveled at the deep contrast of their fingers laced together. The deep dark chocolate to the soft beige contrast of their fingers laced together made his heart cramp. She smoothed one of her hands across his wrist and tears sprung to his eyes.

"Tissue paper. "He hazarded a glance at her.

Twin pools of the deepest green shifted slowly over his face as they had all those years ago in the interrogation room at the Shadow Bay Police Precinct. The agonizing, tormenting slowness with which she took in his features still stripped him bare. She raised an eyebrow, as if to question.

"Your hands are tissue paper soft." Cass focused on her hands once more then cleared his throat.

He ran his thumbs over her printless palms. The one distinguishing characteristic, a fine scar that could have easily been a lifeline had it not been so jagged.

"Did it hurt?"

Alana's gaze drifted over his fingers tracing the scar as her face clouded over. "No, but it bled for a long time afterward. I had to wear extra gloves for a while. Couldn't leave any DNA on scene during the heists." A sad smile whispered over her features. "You stayed with me; endured my meltdown.... You kissed me and as much as I wanted you to, my knee jerk reaction was to fight. I never meant to scare you."

Cass bit down on his lip and shook his head.

"We were both scared, Alana. Scared to live, but not scared to die." he said quietly.

"The grief gets heavy. Your resolve buckles and as horrific as it sounds it almost seems rational."

He watched as she ran her finger over the gnarled scar on the web between his thumb and forefinger. He cleared his throat before venturing another look at her. As always, her gaze was steady on him.

"You want the pain to end. Some prayers you back away from. Some prayers you answer for yourself. I never replaced the mug I broke that night at your apartment."

Cass raised one of her hands to his mouth. It trembled as her finger rested against his lips. "Alana, I meant... your fingerprints." Cass swallowed at the lump forming in his throat.

Alana moved to take her hands away, and he stilled them. She took in a slow breath and settled back in her chair.

"Knox thought if he shot me up with enough heroin maybe I wouldn't feel it. Isla was scared. My heart had stopped. I felt every second of the acid washes. My fingerprints were stubborn. There were nine acid treatments in all, but by then I'd forgotten how to scream."

"Jesus..." Cass jerked his hands away so quickly that he upset her cup of coffee, making it spill on her hand.

"Are you alright?" Alana plucked the discarded napkin from Gabe's bowl and sopped at the mess.

"I damn near scald your hand and you're asking me if I'm okay?" Cass yanked the dishtowel from the oven door and wrapped her hand in it. "Isla...Knox? Who are these people?"

"Isla Ado and Harvey Knox were my handlers. Dominic didn't trust himself to be alone with me at first. After watching your brother die, I begged him to kill me. Dominic refused." Her gaze grew distant as she winced at some private pain. "Dominic sent me and a few others overseas to train with them for training. Some died, others were nearly driven insane. I was the only one that finished."

Cass shook his head sharply as he dried her hand and tried to wrap it in the dishcloth. "You never... I don't remember you ever talking about any of this, you never said...."

"You asked me not to tell you anymore that first night."

Cass looked up at her, his eyes flooding with recognition. "The first time we made love was twelve years ago. In all that time you never said anything."

"I did what you asked." She shrugged and rolled up her sleeve.

He glanced at the scar she'd shown him to comfort him all those years ago, because at the time he was ashamed of the scars on his hands.

His mind clouded with the memory of measuring the milk in the glasses before pushing the one with the most over to her as they dined on peanut butter and banana sandwiches. Cass put his hand out to stop her, before pushing her sleeve higher. He ran his thumb along the jagged line.

"You were so gentle, running your hands over my scars... trying to erase them or maybe work your compassion, your empathy into them.

After a while I just accepted that pain was all I would ever know."

"Until me..."

Alana nodded as she pulled away. She took the cloth from around her hand and sopped up the pool of coffee spreading under the sugar bowl and the napkins. She walked over to the sink to rinse out the cloth.

"Yes, Cassiel, until you."

"Alana, are you leaving me?"

CHAPTER 6

Alana turned on him so quickly that he blinked and sat back. "What?"

"Am I going to come home and find you and Gabriel gone?" His tone was civil, but a thread of annoyance chilled the air.

"I would never take our son from you." Alana walked over and handed him a clean dishtowel.

"But *you're* leaving? Is that what you're telling me?"

Alana reached out to touch him, and Cass sat back out of her reach.

"Don't Alana. You know I can't think straight when you touch me."

Alana stepped back, and he grabbed her hand.

"Wait…. I sorry. I didn't mean… Look just tell me…. please." He dropped her hand and scrubbed his face. "Are you leaving me?"

Alana studied him for what seemed like an eternity before she reached for him again.

Cass moved to shrug her off then stopped. He struggled not to moan as rested a hand against his neck. Alana ran her thumb over his pulse then hooked a finger under his chin and made him face her.

"Are you leaving *me*, Cassiel?"

He tilted his head as if seeing her for the first time. "How could you even ask me that?" he said in an anguished whisper. "You are the only one I want to grow old with."

Alana moved his mug and sat down on the table directly in front of him. "Do you remember what you said to me on our wedding night?"

Cass tried to stand, but Alana easily blocked his path. He sat down hard and scrubbed the place between his eyebrows with the heel of his hand. "That has nothing to do with—"

Alana took his face in her hands and silenced him with a kiss. He groaned as he pulled her down onto his lap. She pulled back from him and ran her thumb over the scar and then over his bottom lip. "Answer me."

Despite the fleece that swam all around her, her nipples ached against the rasp of fabric.

"Alana." Cass tried to focus on the lettering on the sweatshirt, but his eye fell to the scar traveling from her collar bone down to her breast.

"Do you remember?" She repeated.

He tried to get up once more, and she folded her legs around his waist.

"Alana…. Don't use your body against me."

"Why not? It's what you did to me upstairs. Answer me."

Again, he attempted to stand, but Alana took his face in her hands and kissed him.

Cass let his hand fall to her hip to brace her as she rocked gently on his thighs. "Answer me. What was the pact we made on our wedding night?"

"Nobody leaves." He moaned, deepening the kiss.

"That's right, nobody leaves. I have given you the option more than once. Even as I gave birth to our son, I gave you an out. I had papers drawn up that forfeited my parental rights just like I did with Monet."

He grabbed her hips and shook her once.

"And I tore them up. Stop it." He searched her face. "I mean it."

"I never wanted to inflict myself or my demons on you." Alana leaned forward and pressed her forehead against his.

"Babe, stop. Please. You're not some kind of assault." Cass took her face in his hands.

"I've done things. People like me dream of a happily ever after. On the outside, it's perfect. On the inside, it's my worst nightmare."

"Nightmare, why?"

"The devil will have his due. Memories are long. I was a whore, a thief, a murderer in some people's eyes. And worse, I was a snitch. People don't forget; not when there's money involved. You saw the ad for me on the Dark Web."

Cass moved to speak, and she kissed him hard and deep. Alana gripped his hand and pushed it down to cup her breast before she slipped his hand down the front of her sweatpants. His eyes widened as the hot, slippery feel of her covered his fingers. Cass tried to remove his hand, and she tightened her grip around his waist. His fingers slid into her, and she ground her hips against him as she moaned against his ear.

"You name it: people, drugs, oil, art, jewels. Did you really think all those jobs I did for you and the government would go unanswered? People made or ended careers off of what I did. I served their purpose, and if I didn't then the threat of losing the children or losing you was all they needed to keep this old marionette dancing.

"That's not...."

"What true, Cassiel?" she finished for him.

Alana released him and sat back far enough to see him straight on. "Is this where we start lying to each other? After everything you witnessed, everything I've done, are you still convinced that all monsters walk on four legs?"

"Alana..."

"I sat in the back of vans listening to men die because they were stupid enough to throw in with Julian. I didn't pull the trigger, but I killed them just the same. We both know what I am." Her smile took on a sad, ancient look as she squeezed his shoulder. "Tell me I'm wrong, I'll believe you."

"We're happy, Alana. I retired from the FBI; we both did. The pipelines changed, the distributors, all of that changed or went underground. We are finally free; we don't want for anything."

Alana blinked, and her eyes were bright with tears. One spilled down her cheek. She hid her face in the warm space between his neck and shoulder. She pressed her trembling lips to his collarbone and then the space just above his ear.

"I wanted my husband to make love to me this morning."

"Alana."

Cass slid his hand up her back and under her hair. He pulled her down and crushed her mouth with his own. Alana molded her body to his, and he reached between her thighs and cupped her sex like it was a wound. He massaged her gently.

"Believe me, I wanted to. Alana, it killed me to get up. I didn't mean to hurt you. I wanted you to level with me."

Alana whimpered against his ear as she fell still against him. "So that's why you tested me?" she whispered.

"What?" Cass asked as he sat back and looked at her.

"After a long assignment, my ex-husband, Julian, would test me the same way. He called it making sure things were intact."

Cass snatched her up by her hips and stood her in front of him. "Do *not* group me with him! Don't you *ever* group me with Julian!" He gave her a savage shake that sent her red hair flying around her head in a storm.

Alana let her head roll back on her shoulders before she looked at him. "Tell me I'm wrong. You know it hurts when you withdraw from me too quickly. She glanced down at his hands. "You've never put your hands on me like this. Tell me I'm wrong."

Cass looked down at his hands in horror and dropped her as if she were hot and walked over to the patio door.

"Julian always did it after a long assignment where he had injected me into situations where he thought he could score. He called it immersion. Heads of state...royalty. I spent some nights in dumpsters and some in the bedchambers of kings. The dumpsters were always better."

"I don't want to hear anymore, please just stop. It's in the past. I'm sorry I brought it up. "He could see her reflection in the patio doors as she turned to clean off the table.

"Which brings us back to my question. Are you leaving me? After everything you know from back then and what I just told you… Are *you* leaving *me*?"

"My question. *I* asked first." Cass answered with an impersonal nod. "And it was a yes or no question."

Alana walked over to the door and rested her forehead between his shoulders. When Cass arched his back to get away from her. Alana seized on the opportunity to wedge herself between him and the patio door so that she was looking up at him.

"Then you should know my answer. After all, scratch a liar, find a thief isn't that right, cop?" She put her hands in the center of his chest and shoved as hard as she could.

"You haven't called me that in years…. Cop. You make it sound like a curse word." Cass fell back a step.

She stopped at the chair their son sat in for breakfast. Her hand was almost hidden by the cuff on the shirt.

"Haven't felt like a suspect in years." She held onto the ornate wooden scrollwork that made up the top of the backrest. Cass crossed the space in three strides.

"For now. "He pressed his face against the back of her neck and breathed her in. "Tell me what you're waiting for? It's what you said last night."

She turned, and he took an involuntary step backward.

"I almost died with you. I laid down my life to bring our son into this world. Scratch a liar." Tears streamed from her eyes. She raked the back of her hand over her cheek.

"Alana, I'm sorry. I didn't mean to make you cry." Cass hugged her from behind and pressed his face into the back of her neck and sighed.

Alana turned and kissed him, smearing her tears on his face. Cass opened his mouth to respond, Alana grabbed his face and shook him.

"Do I taste like a lie?" She inclined her head, daring him. "Answer me. Has my body *ever* lied to you? Scratch a liar…. Tell me, Cop…. Scratch a…."

Cass stepped forward and silenced her with a kiss.

Alana jerked away. "Answer me, Cop." Her chin quivered as she struggled not to cry. She shoved at his chest. "Scratch a liar, Cop."

"Alana stop, babe. I'm sorry." He crushed her to his chest and kissed her.

She sobbed against his mouth, as she let her hands skim over his shoulders and down the collar of his shirt. Cass pushed her sweatpants down and stomped on the crotch.

Alana tugged at his belt buckle belt and zipper, as he moved closer, pushing her up the wall until she was straddling his hips and one of her hands encircled him. The other slid down the back of his jeans as she took the tip of him and scored her hot, slick sex.

One thrust and he was in her. Another and another pushed her up against a small plaque that held the car keys to the wall. She cried out as the key hanger dug into her back. He batted it off the wall as he gripped the doorsill she writhed against. The more she panted the harder he thrust; his mouth pressed against her throat.

Alana wrapped her legs around his hips and matched every thrust with her own. Harder and harder they thrust until Alana cried out and her legs slipped from around his hips. Cass thrust once more and then clung to her as the wicked current of life flowed through them.

"What was our agreement?" she sobbed against his ear. "Say it because I remember."

"Nobody leaves, Alana. Nobody leaves." Cass murmured as he kissed her tears away.

CHAPTER 7

Valerie Banks downed the last of the Everclear Vodka from her skull-shaped shot glass and reached for the bottle. Phaedra, her wife was still sleeping in the gray hours—that time just before the sun touched the sky or decided that this was going to be just another dreary British day.

Phaedra worked hard at being pretty, even in her sleep. From the white blonde braids on her head to the deep dark chocolate brown of her skin, Val's wife was a vision in repose right down to her breast implants and jewel-toned silk nightgowns.

Val glanced at the walk-in wardrobe to her left. Racks upon racks of clothes and shoes sat silently waiting for Phaedra to choose them. Her wife's vanity was crowded by a staggered riser-type case filled with every shade of colored contact lens.

In a few hours, Phaedra would emerge from the bathroom wearing her newest set of eyes, while stroking her waist-length blonde hair like a pet.

Val had long given up trying to imagine who or what would come out of the bathroom. With each pair of eyes or lace-front wig there seemed to be a new personality.

She simply smoothed her own hair back from her honey brown face and pulled on an Italian suit that was tailored to her small stature. Val was secretly grateful for the breast cancer. Two radical mastectomies later, she had the flat chest she'd longed for as a girl. Val wasn't male-she never wanted to be. But being less than female suited her fine.

Phaedra never questioned her, and no one else did either. She eclipsed everybody, making it easier for Val to be there in the background, with a drink in her hand and music etching the bass into her chemotherapy-softened bones. Life had been perfect. They had money. More than enough, but Phaedra wasn't satisfied. Nothing seemed to slake her thirst for more. Riches were more than a God for Phaedra.

Val downed another shot and waited for the buzz that never seemed to find her lately. The medicinal marijuana she had blended into her vanilla cigarillos settled her stomach and took the edge off the pain, but little else. She'd grown accustomed to the pain. At times it was almost bearable. It kept her awake and alert, and in a constant killing mood—which she thoroughly enjoyed.

She looked down at the phone in her lap and watched the patch-in she had to the closed-circuit television. She shrugged, relishing the feel of the leather, tailor-made holster that stretched across her shoulders.

The deadly weight of the two pearl-inlaid handguns the holster held in place near the small of her back made her smile inwardly. Some people clung to their cell phones like a security blanket. The guns did the same for her.

They had, she knew, passed the point of no return when they'd taken the girl from the panic room in her apartment. Phaedra seemed pleased, as if it were the most entertainment she'd had in years.

When the child came around, she didn't look scared. She simply surveyed her surroundings and crouched at the far end of the room with her back pressed against the wall.

Three days in and she hadn't eaten a thing, just stared at the door quietly struggling to stay awake. Val finally had Vincent hold the girl down so they could tranquilize her and give her an IV. It was bad enough they'd taken her. To have Monet die before they could test her to see if she was anything like her mother was out of the question.

Phaedra had a timetable when it came to her cruelty. She was all about punctuality. Things happened in her perfect time and in her perfect order. People had a funny way of dying around Phaedra when things didn't go the way she planned—as Vincent found out.

If anything, the man was more than a loose end. He seemed to take perverse pleasure in taunting Monet. Phaedra caught him playing with the light switch in the girl's cell and told Val about it, laughing while she told her.

Val left her usual seat in the darkest part of the room and found him. She was actually sorry Monet was deaf. Val wanted her to hear him screaming.

Monet... Even her name reminded Val of the girl's mother. Back then Alana was smaller than everybody, yet stronger than all of them. Val closed her eyes against the memory.

The surveillance photos never did Alana justice. Standing outside her Center for Runaways at its grand opening, Alana, as always, seemed to look beyond the camera, across the years, directly at Val.

She'll hate me now. The stark realization made Val sit up in her chair and reach for the vodka once more.

"It sounds so exotic. Imagine a diamond the size and shape of a rolling pin but harder...sharper... Splinter of Heaven. Even the name..." Phaedra rolled over, stretching, almost basking in the whisper of the black satin sheets adorning their bed.

"Kid's not her mother. Told you that. The girl can climb, but you saw her yesterday. She's not her mother. We need to end this, Phaedra, go back to formula." Val needed to say it. Someone needed to say it.

"A life for a life, remember? That was what you promised me.

Alana Symone took something from me, and I returned the favor. If you love me, you'll support me. "She let the black sheet spill from her shoulder, exposing one chocolate nipple.

"If you love me, then I shouldn't have to worry so much about myself. Should I, Valerie? Should I be worrying about myself these days?"

Val stood. "You know better, Phae. Don't step to me like that. I'm not the one. You made us move to this swamp. I was fine in the States."

Phaedra writhed on the bed, pulling the sheets away from her. She inched the scrap of lace that passed for underwear over her hips. From where she stood, Val could see the freshly groomed exclamation point of Phaedra's pubic hair. "I'm sorry, baby. Let me make it up to you."

"You're going to have to do a lot more than that to make it up to me," Val spat.

"Yes, I know you like to fight when we fuck."

"Shut up," Val said, trying hard not to notice as Phaedra's French-manicured fingers disappeared into her slick folds. Val set the shot glass aside and went over to the bed.

"Yes, you want me to fight you, prove to you how much I love you. Besides, you told me you liked Europe. You don't have to travel so far for your suits."

"Shut up!" Val grabbed Phaedra's thigh and nearly dragged her off the bed.

"What makes you angrier, the fact that it's me or that I'm not her? I mean you could have a harem, and it wouldn't be enough, would it? Not unless it was her. I can pretend if it will make you happy. I bought green contact lenses just for the occasion. My back isn't a mess of scars, but we can pretend.... You like to pretend, don't you? I know you love the smell of juniper berries. I know about that bottle of body lotion. Smells like her.... You still rub it all over when you want to fuck her instead of me. She never even kissed you. You don't even know what she tastes like, but it's amazing what she can do to you after all these years... after all this time." Phaedra taunted.

"What did I just say? What the fuck did I just say?!" Val roared.

CHAPTER 8

"Are you okay, Babe? Did I hurt you?" His voice was always soft and quiet afterward.

"Shh, no, Gabe." She whispered.

Alana listened until Cass's ragged breaths evened into a deep slumber. His sweat dried on her skin as she looked out their bedroom window. Morning passed into early afternoon. The pleasant rawness of his whisker burns and the fullness of him still embedded within her made her heart crowd into her throat as the tears slid silently into her hairline.

Their union bordered on violence as the last of his anger and fear gave way to his usual worshipping touch that always summoned the deepest orgasms from her. But the longer she was there with him, the more the dread spilled into her veins. The awful knowing she'd long forgotten was returning with a sickening twist in her gut.

Her ex-husband, Julian, had been dead for years, but it still didn't feel real. Alana heard the reports, but for her it wasn't real until she saw his body with her own eyes. Cass carried her down to the morgue and protested when she asked him to put her down. He crushed her to his chest.

"No. You can see him from here," he murmured in her ear.

"Please, Cassiel," she said.

Cass held onto her for a few seconds more before setting her down, but the alarm was going off in her head just the same. She limped over to the gurney with Cass no more than a step behind her.

She studied Julian's features and the strange look of terror she saw on his face. It was as if whatever he had seen after death was far worse than anything he'd done in life. In a certain light, Julian was almost handsome. She ran a finger over the tear tracks that had dried to pale lines on Julian's face. His skin was cold, but the alarm was going off in her head.

There was always something more she had to do. Julian saw to it. Julian was always planning, but Julian was dead.

Won't hurt after a while. You won't even notice the blood running down your chin when you smile. Broken bones... commonplace... occupational hazard, and the scars? You'll come to treasure them... even be proud of some of them. You'll even come to enjoy it in a sense... welcome it. You told me once that you were proud of the cigar burns and that knife wound on your arm. Do you remember? You may even pick fights with me to restore the balance. Sex, love, and pain. It's what we're all made of in the end.

Julian's words echoed from somewhere deep inside her as she tried to shake the memory. She had hovered over Julian too long for Cass' taste. He swept his arm under her legs and cradled her to his chest.

"It's over, Alana. He can't hurt you anymore," Cass had told her over and over in the ambulance that night. Alana knew what he was saying, believed what he was saying, but it all rang hollow.

With Julian out of the way the ripple effect would be vast. Allies became candidates. Some, like hermit crabs, planned to move into Julian's vacated seat and take over. Others wanted to merge, while even more felt cheated because they weren't the direct cause of death.

Alana barely noticed that she was bleeding from the bullet wound in her shoulder or the broken arm and ankle. The adrenaline pouring into her bloodstream deadened everything.

One minute, she'd been on the roof staring down the barrel of Julian's gun, and the next, she was falling... forever falling—and then the trees seemed to snatch her up short. The branches snapped and clawed at her. At one point her climbing cords wrapped around her neck. Alana barely untangled them before she hit one of the branches, felt her arm bend at an awkward angle, and snap.

She rolled off the branch and landed wrong and felt something pop in her ankle. The waterfall's icy spray made her wounds sting. But none of that mattered. Alana had defied Julian, and he always kept his promises.

Alana remembered casting one last look up at the building while the lights from the helicopters swept over the wooded terrain. Blending into the night was a mercy as she carefully made her way from the woods to the hatchback she had hidden under some brush days ago.

When she arrived at Lydia's house and made her way into Lydia's son Sean's bedroom, she shambled over to the bed to cover both children with the blanket, then spilled into the rocking chair to watch them sleep.

It would have been so easy to walk away. That was the plan if she survived: to live as if she'd died. There were places she could go, people who were waiting to give her sanctuary.

Isla and Knox were in France; Val was at the airport with Whispers and Phaedra. Val, with her cancer-ridden frame, was waiting. Her black backpack was probably filled with gauze and anything else she thought Alana would need. And then it would be off to Europe. Val knew of places and would be more than willing to help her cease to exist. She could still hear Val pleading with her in her soft, raspy voice.

"Let me take care of you, Alana. Let me try. Leave all this behind. You know five-oh won't let you rest. I have places we can go. Libraries we can get lost in. Be dead to them...all of them. They don't deserve you. They never did."

Part of Alana knew Val was right. She needed to be dead to the world and even to herself for a while. It was the only way to be sure. Julian was dead, but the people he was in league with were not. Alana could hurt them. Badly. And then anyone and everyone around her would pay.

He would take care of her daughter. He would love Monet better than any father could. She'd watched as Lydia doted over Sean and knew the woman would help Cass care for Monet. Alana was all set to leave when she felt Monet's gaze on her.

Then Sean was out of the bed, heading downstairs, and Cass was there, asking her to come home to him. Not simply to a place with four walls, but to come home to *him*.

Was it possible?

Alana could hear herself asking him if he knew how much she loved him. She'd meant it as an explanation. She'd meant it as a way of saying goodbye, but the more she looked at him and felt the warmth of Monet tucked down against her side it all fit together.

Here was her chance... the sliver of peace she longed for... that last best chance for her to come in from the cold. The quiet desperation in Cass's voice, the way he touched her... loved her. Alana wasn't even sure when or how she slid to the floor into his arms. All she knew was that he'd held onto her from that day on.

Alana smoothed a hand over Cass's back, and he snuggled even closer. She wrapped her arms and legs around him where he rested between her thighs and tried to drink in every facet of him. Cass belonged to her. He'd moaned it in her ear more than once, but as he rested against her, suddenly his simple statement took on a deeper meaning.

If Alana died, he wouldn't be able to go on living. He'd said it once before, and at first she thought it was just something people said. But as the laugh lines in his face deepened and the crow's feet around his eyes blossomed, she knew that if old age embraced her and death remembered where she was, Cass refused to survive her. He'd get the children through childhood, but then… Alana knew.

Cass would simply stop living and follow her.

Alana felt him stretch against her, and she relaxed her embrace so that he could move. She smiled at the feel of his warm mouth as he left soft sucking wet kisses across her chest until he found one of her nipples. Cass leaned up so that he could kiss her once more, and she slid her hands down to his backside and urged him closer.

CHAPTER 9

Cass dried his hands on the towel draped over his shoulder as he eyed his cell phone on the counter. Alana had gone to pick up their son, leaving him alone in a house that seemed to be devoid of life. He walked over to the phone and watched it jitter across the counter.

The number on the caller ID dropped a dose of adrenaline into his blood. He looked up at the ceiling, then grabbed the cell phone and pressed the call button. It didn't dawn on Cass until that moment, but for years whenever he saw Nicholas Levine's name in the caller ID on his phone, he would look up at the ceiling as he tried to will away the queasy feeling that toyed with his gut.

"Patrick Cohn died of prostate cancer a while back. I thought I'd seen the last of this number then."

"Believe me, I wish you never had to see it again. I'm at the front door," Levine said before the line went dead.

Suddenly Cass wanted Alana in front of him, smiling softly as she studied him. They'd spent the entire morning and most of the afternoon making love. When she moved to get dressed, Cass found himself clinging to her. He'd almost offered to go with her to pick up their son, but after showering with her and making love again, Alana gently pushed him back into the kitchen to start on the salad and the spaghetti sauce. Cass was in the middle of spinning the last of the water from the salad greens when the phone rang.

Cass opened the door to see Levine standing there, looking as haggard as he remembered. Both men were the same age and yet Levine always looked older, as if The Job had sapped his youth. Cass leaned against the door without inviting him in.

"Alana gave you people everything she had. For ten years we gave you the best we had and still you dog her every step. What is it you think she knows now?" Cass fixed the cuff on one sleeve of his plaid flannel shirt. "You want her to pick some high-tech lock, or tell you how to get into the bedchamber of some drug czar without being detected? She doesn't do that anymore. She hasn't for a long time, so why don't you people just..."

"Monet is missing, Cass."

Alana glanced in the rearview mirror at her son as they pulled out of the Wal-Mart parking lot. Gabriel's head was buried in a gaming magazine as he hummed along to some song that emanated from the white dual cords of his ear buds. She looked back at the road and at first she thought she was seeing things. Cass' medallion, the one she herself had worn for a while before asking him to give it to her daughter, turned lazily as it hung from the rearview mirror.

Alana looked back at her son. Panic made for poor planning. Terror gave the illusion of time. Pain spawned purpose and clarity, making everything clear. After all there was a time when apologies were petty in her line of work. Alana made her way further and further away from the city limits and closer to home.

After the latest snowstorm, the side streets were passable. The plows had cut a path that sent whatever blanketed the streets to both sides of the road. Salt and ash had colored the once white snow the cruel gray of hardpack.

"Gabriel, honey, put your new coat on."

"But, Mom, it's hot in here already."

"Now, Gabe. Please."

One look in her eyes and he wordlessly unbuckled his seat belt and pulled the coat out of the bag. He started pulling off his old coat.

"No, put the new one on top of that one. Do it now, Gabe. Get rid of the earphones. Where are your gloves? Put them on." Alana glanced at the rearview mirror to see the high beams from a truck coming up behind them. "Where's your hat? Get that seat belt back on, Gabe!"

No sooner had she said the words, than the truck behind them surged forward, slamming into them. Alana stomped on the breaks as they hit a patch of black ice and began to fishtail across the road.

Above the crunch of metal and the screeching tires, all she could hear was Gabriel screaming.

CHAPTER 10

"A lot of things aren't clear at the moment, Cass." Levine watched as Cass paced back and forth punching the number 1, his speed dial number for Alana. The one and only selfie he'd taken of them together flashed on the screen. He was looking into the camera, but Alana was fast asleep with her face pressed into his neck. Her red hair spilled across his chest like an exotic silk scarf.

"What's clear to me is that my daughter has been missing for seventy-two hours, and we're just now getting word."

"At first we just figured she was off somewhere with her boyfriend. She did that sometimes."

"Monet always checked in with us."

"Not if she had a boyfriend."

"I'm not naïve, Nicholas. Monet had at least two that I know of, and one she's slept with."

"Not if he was assigned to protect her." Levine shook his head and looked away.

"Wait... what did you say? You... Mo was only supposed to have female guards. That was the agreement when Alana did that last gig for you people." Cass took a step back as fearful images filled his mind. "Oh my God, what did you people do?"

"New management. They didn't have coverage one night and the next thing you know... Cass it doesn't matter. Vincent Roark is dead. They found him about an hour ago in his apartment. Eyes gone. Throat slashed. It was a secondary crime scene. Not enough blood and whatever was left was settling."

Cass felt the energy spill from his legs as he sat down hard in the chair. "I don't give a damn about... wait... the panic room. How did Mo..."

"Closed-circuit shows that she made it into the panic room you had built into her apartment. After that, everything went dead. Cameras, the door—even the telephone and the alarm, which is why you never got word." Levine folded his hands and rested his mouth against them.

"Hell, *we* didn't know until we broke down the door looking for her. Couple of her professors said she always reported to class. According to one of them, Monet never missed tests."

Gabriel's words from that morning took on a newer, more painful feel. He rubbed the place on his forehead where his son had tapped him. He knew what his son was saying, but he knew what Alana meant.

"My daughter had two cell phones. I put burners in the safe in the panic room, along with cash and her gun."

"Burners were still there. No sim cards. One of her phones was shattered. The other we pinged the towers around her apartment and got nothing. Cass, we are doing everything in our power. Mistakes were made, and I take full responsibility."

"Is this where you end your perfectly crafted statement with the words *and I'm sorry*? Is that supposed to make me feel better?"

He watched Levine shake his head and look away. Just then, Cass' phone rang in his hand. "Babe, where are you?"

"Cass, it's me, Mark."

"Mark, why are you calling me from my wife's phone?"

"I need you to come down to the Barrens. There's been an accident."

CHAPTER 11

Tarmac at BWI/ Thurgood Marshall Airport

Val felt her phone vibrate against the bandages wrapped around her chest. A jolt of excitement warred with the nausea that twisted her gut.

She's home, she thought.

The prospect softened Val's usual scowl. In the past, all it took to set her straight was one look at her, one breath of her hair. Val took in a breath that made her insides shudder. She moved to sit up, and her stomach cramped. A warm hand fell to her shoulder, and at last Val opened her eyes to see her doctor staring down at her. His salt and pepper hair glowed under the florescent light of the airplane hangar.

"You still have at least an hour of infusion left, Valerie."

Val reached over and closed the chamber on the IV. She unscrewed the port and sealed the one attached to her chest.

"Wasted breath I see."

Val sat up on the bed and let her legs dangle. She glanced up to see the doctor give some silent instruction to one of the nurses. Val eased herself to the floor and assumed her full height. She buttoned her shirt over the port, and as she shrugged into her gun holster she heard the commotion coming up the hall.

"Bullet wounds: one to the left arm and one to the head. Deep lacerations, contusions, breaths shallow, we need to get a film on her midsection and her right ankle and those head injuries. What the hell were you guys doing out there? Val said no blood, no sound!"

"She put up a fight...."

Val looked down at the charcoal grey suit jacket but reached for her lab coat instead. As she rounded the corner leading into the makeshift triage room, her heart sank. Medical personnel were dashing about, moving Alana's body from one gurney to another, being careful not to move the cervical collar or the backboard too much. Val started across the floor.

"Cut her out of those clothes and handcuff her to the railing. Injured or not, that bitch worse than a cornered rat."

Val jerked to a stop as Phaedra walked past her, smoothing a hand over her shoulder as she went.

Phaedra slowly made her way around the gurney, taking in Alana's nude body. The doctor and his two nurses busied themselves with assessing Alana. At one-point Phaedra shoved one of the nurses out of the way before she ran a long, French-manicured nail over the ragged bikini-cut scar that marred Alana's tight midsection.

"Here's a new one. That's not a bikini cut though. Wasn't there a baby, a boy, I think? He would be about..."

"Gabriel is seven, almost eight. Phae, I need to get in here, can you just... stand over there somewhere? I need to know how bad she is." Val murmured as she worried the blanket she clutched to her chest.

"Don't get too close, Val; you don't know where she's been."

"Alana's not dirty, Phaedra."

"She could be covered in mud and shit, and you'd probably say the same damned thing. In case you've forgotten, chemotherapy leaves you compromised." Phaedra peered at Val over her shoulder, and Val rolled her eyes and looked away. "And you still had an hour left of that infusion."

"Alana's not dirty, and we were talking about her son."

She shoved passed Phaedra hurriedly and put the warming sheet over Alana, being careful not to cover her face. She let her fingers grace the side of Alana's neck, searching for a pulse.

Val turned her gaze on the doctor standing with his arms folded and jerked her head in his direction. He ushered his nurses forward as he picked up where he left off. Val swallowed hard then turned around, spreading her arms out along the railing, effectively blocking Phaedra from getting to the gurney.

"We need to work, Phae."

Phaedra moved to step forward, and Val flattened herself against the gurney and looked away.

"Boy's probably, small like her... then again maybe he's like his father. Is the boy here?" Phaedra looked over at the men standing near the door.

"We lost them down around the pilings. She drove straight for the black ice. She spun out and before we knew it, we all lost control. She hit a tree, and we almost plowed in after her. The boy won't survive the elements or the animals, alone in the woods." One of them said.

"You left her baby out there?" Val turned to look at the speaker. "Did you even look for him?"

"We had her. We figuered he was dead already." He fell silent and looked away. "We heard sirens." He said as he looked at his partner for help.

Phaedra walked over to them.

"Pity. He would have been useful." Phaedra glanced back over her shoulder. "I bet she'd do anything to keep her boy safe."

The deadness Val saw in her wife's eyes made her reach for Alana's shoulder. She smoothed a hand over Alana's forehead, moving her hair back from the gash she found there.

"Val is right. You should have searched for him. Val, you are coming?" Phaedra asked as she paused near the door. "They can patch her up. We need to be in the air."

Val took in a deep breath, trying hard not to flinch as she gripped the railing near Alana's head.

"Phaedra, I need to finish in here."

"Brian and the others searched the stream. Nobody could survive those elements, certainly not a kid." One of the men piped up.

Val looked at the man.

"We'll circle back to this fuck-up later. For now, get them out of my sight." Val waved a nurse over as she moved closer to Alana's head.

"We both know he's no ordinary kid, Val. Hell, maybe we should have grabbed him. He's small enough. She trained him. Besides, you saw what her daughter did when she tried to escape." Brian, Val's brother, stripped out of his coat as he walked into the room and came up to the gurney.

Val closed her eyes against the memory of Monet climbing a seemingly smooth wall without effort. She was halfway out of the window when one of Phaedra's men fired on her. Val turned on the man and planted her switchblade in his eye, then leaned down to wipe her blade on his shirt.

"I said use tranquilizers!" she hissed before she walked in to assess Monet's wounds.

Val tried to shake away the memory of Monet falling back inside, and the way her blood ran down the soft peach-colored wall. Val smoothed an imaginary wrinkle out of the warming blanket.

"Brian, since when do we abduct or kill children?" Val noticed Phae standing in the doorway." When was that ever a part of the plan Phae? He's just a little boy."

"Collateral damage, my love. Take enough from this one, break her down to her least common denominator, and she'll do her fancy little dance. She'll do anything for her loved ones; you ought to know."

"Phaedra shut up about that," Val warned.

"Never seen somebody so ready for their big-time appointment with death, miss it so many times."

Phaedra walked back over and used her hip to bump the doctor aside as she yanked back the blanket and dug her fingers into the bruise she saw blooming on Alana's ribcage. Val watched Alana's heart monitor spike before she slipped back into oblivion and Phaedra walked out of the room.

"Have someone finish cleaning her up. She smells like dead leaves. Dead or alive, we're in the air in thirty minutes."

CHAPTER 12

Val swallowed the rage boiling in her throat as she smoothed the blanket back into place. One of the nurses reached over to touch Alana, and Val turned on her.

"Get the fuck out of here. All of you, just go." A dizzy spell seized Val making her hug the bed railing until the world settled once more.

"Prelims aren't back yet. We haven't even…." The nurse complained as she turned to the doctor packing some supplies back into their shipping crates.

She moved to say something else and the doctor gripped the nurse by her arm and pulled her toward the exit the door. "Val *is* a doctor. She can handle the rest."

Val waited until they were out of the room before lifting the blanket. Alana's midsection was riddled with bruises; Val found the one where Phaedra had dug her fingers and covered the place with her hand.

Alana's emerald eyes opened. She searched the room around her before at last turning her head to look at Val.

"There she is. There's my girl." Val took in a deep breath and smiled as she smoothed an errant lock of red hair back from Alana's face.

"Val?" Alana moved to touch Val's face, but the sound of the handcuff drew both of their gazes to Alana's hand.

Val reached in her pants pocket and withdrew the switchblade. She stabbed it into the lock gave a sharp twist, and the cuff opened.

"My husband asked me what I was waiting for. Couldn't tell him... didn't know at the time. Just heard the alarm going off in my head."

"Give Phae what she wants, and it will all be over, Alana." Val gently covered her with another blanket and slid a pillow under her head.

"Searching the dark... always searching the dark. Waiting... forever waiting." Alana shook her head softly. Tears slid across her temples, wetting her hair.

Val brushed the back of her hand over the shimmering tear tracks. She bit down on a curse as tears threatened what little resolve she had left. Lowering the railing, she pressed her forehead against Alana's neck, forcing her to lie still.

"Alana, are you listening to me? Give Phaedra what she wants."

"Don't know what she wants, Val. I never knew what she wanted."

Alana tried to sit up but cried out, reaching for her mid-section.

Val eased her back down to the bed and covered her once more. She pressed her forehead against Alana's, swallowing hard at the lump forming in her throat.

"Splinter of Heaven, Alana. Bigger than the Hope Diamond."

"I don't have it, Val. Even if I did or knew where it was, Phaedra would kill me either way. Someone needs to. I'm tired, Val. So tired of having to pay over and over. Can't do it anymore." Alana began to writhe on the bed as silent sobs shook her body.

"Alana, don't. Shh don't." Val stripped out of the lab coat and draped it over Alana before pressing her chest down against Alana's to hold her still.

And the world fell away.

Alana was there, right in her arms. Nothing else mattered. Not the stones, not even Phaedra. This was the woman she'd bandaged all those years ago.

This was the friend that refused to accept my cancer diagnosis was a death sentence.

The sound of the handcuff clacking against the railing snapped her back to reality. Val grabbed her switchblade and stabbed the other lock. When she was done, she looked down at Alana blinking softly. She turned her head so that she could get a better look at Val.

"The cancer...?"

Val ran a gentle hand over Alana's hair. Then she took Alana's hand and placed it on the bandages. "Took my tits and my hair. Took a minute, but now I can at least make a ponytail. You haven't changed, Alana. In all the years, you are exactly how I remember."

"And Phaedra...? You always said you wanted a home... someone to take care of."

"You were supposed to come to France. I waited for you." Val's eyes grew hard. "We had a plan."

Val walked around the gurney and busied herself with gathering the supplies she needed to wrap Alana's ribs.

"Plans change, Val."

Val gripped the table and let the rage wash through her.

"Mine didn't, Alana. Mine *never* changed. You told me to buy the tickets. You said I didn't have to reschedule anymore. Told me you were coming with me. I made a way for you... for us." Val's voice grew thicker, quieter as the rage seemed to choke out all reason. "You lied to me."

"Even if I had come to you. I could never be what you wanted.... or deserved." Her voice was so soft, and yet Val heard every word, as always.

"None of that shit matters now." Val cleared her throat and continued to rearrange the supplies on the tray. "You've got work to do."

Val felt the heat of Alana's hand resting on the center of her back just above the butt of the guns. It took everything in her to remain on her feet.

"Don't touch me. Alana."

"White lab coat and guns.... strange combination."

"Why? I'm your cut person. Always was, always will be. The education and the guns were your gifts. One to get me paid, the other to protect you."

"No, Val, those guns were to protect you. I wanted you to make a choice."

"I did. Alana. You *know* I did." Val turned and saw a runnel of blood coursing from Alana's mouth.

Val blinked, and the mask of rage that had contorted her features dissolved into a mask of concern. She blindly reached for the gauze and tried to sop up the blood, but Alana blocked her hand.

"Stop.... let me see it. Tony get in here!"

"I'm sorry, Val." Alana gurgled.

Val blinked rapidly as she gently, but firmly, pushed Alana's hand down and away from her face.

"Don't you dare. Not to me. Not after what I've done." Val pressed her face down against Alana's face. "She's alive, Alana, Monet is here. She was wounded when she tried to escape, but I stitched her up.

Val leaned back and continued to try and stem the blood spilling from Alana's mouth. "Your son... I don't know. My people searched. Is he safe? Did you train him too? Did you hide him? Just shake your head if he's safe."

Alana's gaze hardened as she nodded once, and Val let out a sob of relief.

"Okay. Alana, what is the Splinter of Heaven? Do you know what Phaedra is talking about?"

Val watched as Alana searched the ceiling, tears spilling back into her hairline again, as she struggled to remain awake.

"They're only tears now… blood and tears, nothing more.... like me......"

Val looked up at the doctor and nurse coming back into the room.

"Give Phaedra what she wants. Alana, please, are you listening to me?" Val looked down to see she was unconscious.

CHAPTER 13

The freezing rain lent a cruel bite to the air. When Cass got to the Barrens it took three men to keep him from going to the wreckage in the stream. Once the techs were finished, Cass and Mark walked down to the scene. The lights were up, and they created a patch of daylight in the darkness.

From where they stood, Cass could see the blood on the steering wheel and Gabe's water-logged book bag in the back seat. Cass turned to Mark and gripped his shoulders. "Where is my family, Mark? Did they get them out? I mean where's the ambulance. Alana got out. She had to... maybe they're in the woods, is somebody searching? Answer me!"

Just then, the local sheriff walked up to them; the shower cap he wore over his hat glistened with rain that was beginning to freeze.

"Mr. Garrett, let me just say that we are doing everything we can to find the bodies of..." he looked over at Mark, who shook his head once.

"My family isn't dead. Do you hear me, they're not? Tell him, Mark."

The sheriff looked back and forth between Cass and Mark. "Sir, the temperature is well below freezing. The wreckage was nearly submerged when we arrived. The water alone... No one could survive under these circumstances."

"You don't know my wife." Cass shook his head, "No you're not listening to me." Cass backed away from the men searching the area behind them.

"We've been out here grid sweeping for a while now. We have our best body recovery units on standby downstream," the sheriff continued.

Cass grabbed the man by his coat and shook him into a gasping silence. "What did I just say? They are not dead! They're not! Alana would know what to do."

"Maybe not if she was hurt," the sheriff said, gently, but firmly, brushing Cass's hands from his coat.

"Doesn't matter. Alana would never let anything happen to our son. She's careful with us." Cass said. "You don't know my wife."

Gabriel's simple truth from that morning came back to him with a vengeance. Cass looked over to see Levine directing his own men to fan out and start searching.

"Sir, I know this is a difficult situation." The sheriff stepped in front of Cass to steer him back into their conversation. "Do you understand what I am telling you, sir?"

Cass waved the man off and started backing away. "You don't know my wife."

"Sir, I hear what you are saying, but we have to face the very real possibility that the search will end badly. The blood on the steering column, your son's belongings in the back seat... Hypothermia sets in in less than 15 minutes. For children it's less than that. And then there's this..." The sheriff raised a hand, and the deputy standing near the tent they'd erected walked over holding a large, clear evidence bag.

Cass looked down at the coat in the bag. He felt his legs almost give out. Mark gripped his shoulder.

"Sir, is this your wife's coat?"

Cass backed away from both men. His eyes were riveted to the blood that covered the arm of the coat. "You don't know my wife. You don't understand. She's... You don't know my wife." Cass staggered back down toward Levine and the water-logged truck. "Mark, tell him."

* * *

Mark walked over to the sheriff who looked at him with concern. "Chief Brown... Mark, your friend seems so adamant when there's no possible way his wife or son could be alive. You know how these things go. He makes his wife sound as if she..."

Mark ran a hand over his mouth before he looked over his shoulder at his colleague. "Let me put it to you this way, Gene. She is. Whatever Cass thinks... whatever you don't think... My buddy and I both know that she is."

"What?" Gene shrugged.

"Alive." Mark shook his head when the sheriff gave him a look of misgiving. "Ever hear people talk about The Grail or The Case?" he asked. "Cass's wife wrote it. Same woman, this little scrap of a thing, stood up and took cop killer rounds for him. Saved my life too if you really wanna know. Had every reason to let me bleed to death, but she didn't—this was *after* I pulled a gun on her. So whatever Cass thinks she is best at, trust and believe, this girl can do it. Whether it's surviving getting shot or walking away from that wreck over there. Her ability to survive scares the shit out of me, but if anyone can do it, she can, and I'm certain her son is right there with her."

The man looked at Mark and moved to say something.

"I know how it sounds. But if Cass says she's alive then she is."

The sheriff looked over Mark's shoulder to see Cass and Levine's men moving off towards the woods, shouting, *"Alana... Gabe!"*

"So the feds don't bother to introduce themselves?"

Mark clapped the man on his shoulder and shook his head. "See that man over there? That's Section Chief Nicholas Levine. He's in charge of the men you see fading into the woods. But brass tacks? Those men and women aren't here for him. They're here for Cass." Mark fastened his coat and pulled on his gloves.

"That's Cass and Alana's team out there. After Cass left the force, he and Alana joined the Feds and led the group you see out there. Come on, he's not waiting for you and neither am I."

* * *

The further away from the water they traveled, the colder it seemed to get. Even the flashlight beams sweeping and cutting through the darkness and the intermittent sounds of people calling Gabriel's name offered little comfort to Cass.

Local law enforcement stopped calling Alana's name the further away from the lights they walked. At first, Cass continued to call her name, but after a while, the strange current that flowed between them vanished. Cass tripped over an overgrown root and fell to his knees in the snow. His throat felt raw as he struggled not to cry.

"Oh my God, Alana, please. I know you hid him. You'd never let anything happen to him. Please..."

Just then, Cass heard movement in the tree above him. Cass looked up at the bitter blue-black of night.

"Dad?"

Cass frantically searched the snow for his flashlight before he bounded to his feet and panned the beam above his head. "Gabe?"

The little boy blinked and raised his grubby, gloved hand to shield his eyes from the beam. "Where's Mom?"

"Mark! Somebody help me!" Cass yelled. Suddenly, every flashlight was aimed up at the little boy huddled against the tree trunk.

Cass could hear the policemen shouting for ladders as the federal agents closed in on him and formed a perimeter around the tree. Some of the police officers were yelling for the boy to stay where he was. Gabriel hugged the tree tighter and pressed his face into the bark and moved higher up on the branch.

"Would all of you just *shut the fuck up*? Cass, can you reach him?" Mark yelled.

Cass started up the tree. "Gabe stay where you are. Okay? I'm gonna come get you."

"It's okay, Dad. Mom taught me." Gabriel eased himself around so that he could drop his legs to the branch below him.

"Gabe stay where you are. Gabe, wait!"

Gabriel glanced over his shoulder then let go of the branch and plummeted into Cass's arms. Cass released the branch he was holding on to as he folded his body around his son. He landed on his back, clutching his son to his chest.

"Oh my God... Hey, bud! Where'd you learn to climb like that, huh? Didn't you hear me say wait?" Cass rifled through his son's coats. Cass managed to get his son's hat off, and the boy's shock of reddish-brown, curly hair filled his hands. Cass sat there rocking his son back and forth as he continued to check Gabriel over for cuts. "Where are you hurt, bud? Where's all this blood coming from?"

Gabriel squirmed in his father's embrace. "We crashed into the tree. Somebody was shooting at us. Mommy got hit. We got to this tree, and Mommy told me to climb. She told me to stay there until you came for me. She made me stay here." Gabriel burst into tears and buried his face in his father's shoulder.

CHAPTER 14

"He's got some scratches on his forehead from climbing the tree, but other than that he's fine. The doctors said if he hadn't been bundled up in two coats, he would have died from exposure. Alana saved his life." Cass glanced over his shoulder at the staircase Gabriel had climbed, moments before.

Lydia folded her arms around herself and began to pace. Her husband, Richard, tried to put a comforting arm around her, but she waved him off. "And the blood?"

"Alana's. They matched it. She was hurt but must have buttoned him into his coat and carried him away from the stream, shoved him up onto the first branch and told him to climb the rest of the way. She'd sewn granola bars and water into his old coat. "Cass unzipped the hidden pocket he'd watched Alana sew into the hem of their son's coat months ago. "Not that he ate anything." Tears pricked his eyes as two granola bars and a small flat container of water spilled into his hands.

"If it hadn't been for her, none of this would be necessary." Lydia retied the belt to her robe and folded her arms.

Cass turned to look at her. "What?"

Richard reached for Lydia, and she gave him a withering look.

"I knew this would happen. At first, I figured maybe you'd get her out of your system once they put her in prison, but no." She continued to pace back and forth casting glances at the staircase."

"You go off and join the FBI to be closer to her. Sure, they wanted you for the Agency for years. But the only way you'd take the promotion was to be near her? A common thief, a common little... Then to make matters worse, the minute she walks out of prison, you marry her. Well, look at what it's cost you: your career, the respect of your former colleagues, and for what? Then tonight you almost lose your son, all because of your precious Alana."

"It's because of *her* that he's still alive. She taught him well."

Lydia rounded on him. "Did you know I found a survival kit in the bottom of Gabe's book bag once? He had a smartphone, snacks, first aid kit."

"Gabriel was in scouts, you know that."

"Not the way that kit was set up. Sean was an Eagle Scout. He worked with the younger ones like Gabe. But he never carried a switchblade. Not a Swiss army knife, Cass, but a surgically sharp switchblade. Sean told me about the last fishing trip they all went on with Gabe's troop. The way Gabe's bag was packed, the things he did around the camp. Sean's troop leader is ex-military; I asked him about it, and he agreed. Remember last summer when the rains came and flooded the base camp, Sean said Gabe's troop got turned around somewhere along the trail where the road had been washed out. Instead of the boys getting lost, Gabe got them to high ground. Never cried... never panicked."

"My son is alive because his mother taught him to stay that way. Hell, *I* taught him self-defense. What's wrong with that, Lyddy?"

"Protecting him is a parent's job. Gabriel shouldn't have to protect himself. What's wrong with it? Tell me, Cass, what's *right* with it?" Lydia looked over at a picture that sat on the mantelpiece.

The photo featured Gabriel as a baby. Alana was holding him and Monet, and Cass was holding all of them. Lydia walked over and turned the photo face down, mumbling something under her breath.

"Lydia, that's enough!" Richard said as he shot a look at Cass.

Cass tilted his head softly and took in a deep breath. "Say it again, Lyddy. Don't be shy."

"We've all had a long evening. We'll watch over Gabe for you if you need to head back down to the scene." Richard said as he moved between the siblings.

"I was talking to Lydia. Say it to my face, Lydia. It's not like you've made her feel like part of this family." Cass stared his brother-in-law down, making him move out of the way.

"*She* was involved in your twin's death, but you married her anyway. Being your wife doesn't make her part of *my* family. Mamma never would have approved."

"Mamma had Alzheimer's. What bothered you more, the fact that Mamma liked Alana, or that at times Mamma barely tolerated you? Nothing Alana ever did was right in your eyes. You couldn't parade her around like a charity case. You hated that she held her head up. She never wanted nor needed your approval, but I think you wanted hers. I think you envied her."

"Envy? She's an ex-con. She's a whore. Blackmailing you into being with her."

"Wow." Cass huffed out a sharp laugh. "She said that was how you saw her. I told her she was wrong."

"Am I wrong, Cass?"

Richard reached for Lydia again, and she knocked his hand out of her way.

"Never once did Alana complain," Cass continued harshly, she just built her life, her world, around me and the kids. You know what? This has nothing to do with the fact that my son is alive. I was wrong to bring him here."

He scrubbed the space between his eyebrows with the heel of his hand.

"Alana never had a chance. She wasn't good enough, but the money she made working for the FBI spent well enough when Richard got laid off or when he pissed away the mortgage money on the horses.”

“Now wait just a damned minute.” Richard pushed past his wife.

Cass stepped to him.

“Should I tell Lydia about the time Alana talked one bookie into taking your mechanic’s tools instead of your life?” Cass shifted his foot, making Richard back away, almost knocking his wife over.

“Regulus still wants a piece of you for dropping her name instead of paying your bills.” Cass chuckled and shook his head. “Go on Richard. Tell Lydia how Alana’s past saved you and this house more than once.”

“And that past almost took him from you tonight.” Lydia sniffed as she put an arm around Richard’s waist.

“Correction, that past *saved* his life tonight. Go on, Lyddy, say it.”

“What, that I wish she’d died in that bank all those years ago? Well it’s a moot point now, isn’t it?”

“All right, Lydia, you’ve said enough.” Richard tried to hold her back from Cass, but she jerked away to stand toe to toe with her brother.

“Because you are my sister and I love you, I’ll forgive you this once. Just once. And for the record, Alana stepped into the line of fire for *both of us* or don’t you remember. Oh, that’s right. You were hiding behind the desk.”

“Mommy isn’t dead.” Gabriel’s voice sounded raspy as if he had the beginnings of a cold coming on.

CHAPTER 15

The small white bandage on his forehead was gone. The long, fine scratches looked angry under the house lights. Cass picked him up. Gabriel sighed and tucked his head under his father's chin. Cass looked over at his nephew, Sean, who frantically looked to his parents for help.

"He wanted to see you, Uncle Cass."

Cass smoothed his hand over his son's back before he sat him back from his shoulder. "Hey, bud, you need to be upstairs where it's warm." He pressed his lips to his son's forehead, feeling the beginnings of a fever.

The little boy gripped his father's face and made him look at him. "Did you hear me, Dad? Mom's not dead and neither is Mo. I saw the necklace."

"What necklace?"

Gabe pulled the necklace off and held it up to his father in his pudgy little fist. "Mo's necklace, Dad. The one you gave her when she was little. She never took it off, but it was hanging on the rearview mirror in

Mom's truck. It wasn't there yesterday afternoon. It was there when we left Wal-Mart tonight"

Cass walked over to the sofa and sat down. He draped the necklace back over his son's head. "Start over, Gabe."

"Mom made me swear that if she ever asked me to do anything, even if it didn't make sense, that I would do it no matter what."

"I don't understand." Cass glanced at Lydia and Richard.

"Mom asked me to put my new coat on over my old one."

Mark came back into the living room from taking a phone call. He paused at the sight of all of them staring at the boy.

"Mom taught us how to get away from strangers and how to take care of each other until one of you came for us. She taught me how to make a survival kit, a real one." Tears flooded his eyes, and he scrubbed them away.

"It's okay Bud. Go on." Cass rubbed his son's back as his gaze slid to Mark's face.

The silent message that passed between the two men made Mark venture closer as he dug a small pad of paper and a pen from his coat pocket.

Mom showed me how to get home if I ever got lost, and how to get to Aunt Lyddy and Uncle Richard. She even taught me how to catch the bus to Shadow Bay to Uncle Mark's house."

"They hit us from behind, and we slammed into a tree by the stream. The water was coming in, and the airbag blew up. Mommy got knocked back in her seat. She cut her seatbelt and mine. She banged her head on my door on the glass. She was bleeding, and she wouldn't let me wipe it away. Kept hearing something hitting the leaves and kicking up snow and dirt. We were halfway across the river when she fell. When I looked up, her arm was bleeding." Gabe put a hand on his father's bicep."

Cass took his hand and tried to rub some warmth into it. Gabe's chin quivered.

'Mom kept walking back and forth like she was trying to find something. We saw the flashlights. She gave me the necklace, then held me up so that I could grab the first branch. I couldn't reach it, so she shoved hard and told me to climb." Gabe gulped hard.

" I thought she was coming too, but she backed away from the tree. Mommy told me to be quiet and wait for you. She walked over to them, and they hit her, threw her in the trunk…." Gabriel buried his face in Cass' shoulder and cried.

"Gabe…" Cass smoothed his hand over Gabriel's back, and the boy sat up.

"Mom isn't dead. She told me she would never leave me unless she had to. I wanna go home. I wanna see Mom and Monet. Daddy, please. I want to go home."

*

Cass folded his arms over his chest to try to ease the pain that welled there. He watched as Myra sat on the side of Gabe's bed rubbing his back as he slept fitfully. She looked up at Cass and nodded once, then followed him out into the hallway and closed the door.

"Thanks for being here."

"Mark called me while you were at Lydia's. Cass…"

"Has anyone been acting strange at the center? Anybody following the kids around?"

"You mean like pimps?"

Cass nodded.

"Place isn't listed. Alana insisted on it for the center and for the transition houses along the network she built to get people out of human trafficking." Myra peeked over her shoulder then lowered her voice.

"There was a girl. When Alana left the tables at Delia's Bistro last night."

"I thought she was going to the bathroom. You followed her?" Myra squinted in confusion. "She's given you no reason not to trust her why…"

"Alana didn't go to the bathroom. I found her outside talking to a runaway. She gave her a cup of soup. Never seen this kid before, but one look at me and she was gone."

Myra stroked her chin softly and started to pace the hallway.

"We don't have any new arrivals. I mean, there was one girl. She called herself Ecstasy, but I heard some of the girls call her Stacey. She only came to the center once. I figured Alana had gotten her into one of the transition houses because I haven't seen her in weeks. Cass, we have to face the very real possibility."

Cass shook his head and backed away from her touch. "I can't, My. I can't walk back in that room and tell my son that his mother and sister are dead."

"But what if they are?"

"Don't... please...I can't."

Myra grabbed his arm and pulled him into an embrace. "Alana is my best friend. She doesn't talk a whole hell of a lot, but then she never had to. She loved you and the children, put you all before everything. She would never leave you intentionally."

Cass pulled away and looked back at his son's bedroom door. "She asked me to let her go in the beginning. Begged me to, but I begged her to stay."

"Cass, stop it!" Myra whispered harshly. "Alana loved you and her life with you. She didn't stay by force, you know that. All I'm saying is that we may have to face the possibility."

"I gave her a house, and she made a home. I gave her my seed, and we have Gabriel. We were trying for another baby. You're right, she wouldn't leave that behind; she wouldn't leave me. I asked her that very thing this morning. We made a promise... a pact. Alana wouldn't go back on her word."

Myra put her hand on Cass's cheek and gave him a sad smile. "No, she would never go back on her word to you."

"Cass?"

At the sound of Mark's voice in the stairwell, Cass flinched, and Myra gave his shoulder a reassuring squeeze. "Go on, I'll stay with Gabe."

CHAPTER 16

Cass blinked back tears as he turned and walked downstairs and back into his kitchen. The place had been taken over by Levine's men. Mark was finishing a phone call when Cass walked down the steps. Mark gripped his shoulder and steered him out onto the patio.

"They're still dragging the stream. The temperature is making it difficult to continue. They plan to wrap up anytime now. They'll start up again when the sun comes up."

"She's not out there."

"Cass, I know you want to believe what Gabriel was saying, but we need to face facts."

Cass gripped Mark's shoulder. "I just went through this upstairs with Myra. She's not dead. Why do you think I was able to walk out of the woods tonight? I can't feel her, Mark."

"Cass, I never understood the relationship you two had. It was always stronger than anything I've ever seen, but she's human. The crash... nobody could have survived that wreckage in the front seat without being hurt badly. And you heard Gabe. You saw her coat covered in blood. Only a silencer or suppressor can kick up dirt but not make a whole lot of noise. The cut in her coat is consistent with a gunshot wound. And then a walk through the stream at her size? If the accident and the bullet wound didn't kill her then the cold...Wind chill is in the negatives. Cass, we gotta be realistic."

"Never said she wasn't hurt." Cass swallowed hard before he continued. "I just said she's not in the woods. Gabriel isn't hysterical, Mark. He knows what he saw."

"And what can we do with it? He never saw a face, never saw the make of a vehicle. Hell, we don't even know if it was a car."

"It was a truck, Hummer to be more specific. The paint swatches were matched," Levine said as he came to join them. "We got your wife's truck out of the water and back to our guys." Levine looked at Cass as he spoke, then glanced at Mark. "Your sheriff was none too pleased that I took over, Chief Brown." Levine stuck his hand out to Mark.

Mark shook the man's hand and shrugged deeper into his coat.

"Gene will be fine." Mark said, "He just doesn't like it when others know things and don't share it. He understands that sometimes it's above his pay grade. So, what was in the truck?"

Levine looked back and forth between Cass and Mark. "The blood was a match for Alana. There was some in the front seat, which makes us think she probably got hit with flying glass. Windshield was a mess. Airbag too. Thank God she had her seatbelt on. Gabe was right; it was cut, both of them. Blood on the rear passenger door is also a match."

"What about the tire treads, footprints?"

Levine shook his head. "Cass, when they started the grid sweep, anything that could have been cast was gone. You're right, there was blood in the snow, typed as hers, but no shell casings. I sent Stokes and our photographers back where we found your son. The snow was deep and hard around the tree, which was good for footprints. We matched you and Mark and thought we had matched Alana's, but the pattern was all wrong. It's like she walked around looking for something before she settled on the tree you found Gabe in. Near as we can tell, your wife had to have crossed the stream. Cass, that water was high and hella cold. The current alone should have dragged her off her feet. She covered her tracks that way. We could see where she had stepped back in the same footprints that lead to the tree, her blood was frozen in some of the treads leaving the scene. And then…"

"And then what?" Cass asked.

"She just vanished."

CHAPTER 17

Phaedra watched Val tend Alana's wounds with a reverence that made her blood boil. It bothered her the way her wife cradled Alana close enough to wrap her ribs. Even the way she stitched her wounds seemed more intimate as if in some and stitch the bullet graze to her forehead. Val seemed to be holding Alana's lifeless body a little too close for a little too long. The reverence with which Val seemed to be dressing Alana's wounds made Phaedra seethe inside.

It should have been enough to have Alana cuffed to the bed like an animal. Phaedra had meant to humiliate her by having them cut her out of her clothes, but there was Val, waiting anxiously to cover her and dote on her like she still mattered. It was an old argument between them that always ended with Val yelling, *"Shut up about that. You know what she did. You know why she did it!"*

It wasn't envy. At least that was the lie Phaedra told herself over and over, as Alana seemed to go on with her life after all the damage she'd caused. Alana was no saint. They could at least be clear about that. Val, to her credit, agreed.

No Phae Alana's no saint Never claimed to be. She don't rock her sins like a sable either. She just moved on. Why can't we?

Pride always dripped from the corners of the rare smile Val reserved for whenever she spoke of Alana. No, the wisp of a woman on the gurney wasn't much even after all those years, and yet she still had an effect on Val.

Alana was better than pheromones... better than any of the expensive perfumes Phaedra splashed on that barely got a rise out of Val. Doctors that didn't know Alana from Adam flocked to her side making sure her every need was met. Alana had opened her eyes only once, but Phaedra saw the exchange with Val. The words were muffled, but the attraction was still there. Val had cleared the room. Val wanted Alana to herself.

Phaedra glanced over at the other monitor, to see Val walking from the room that held Alana into the smaller room that held Monet. The girl was sitting up in her bed clutching her thigh as she stared at the door. When Val approached the bed, Monet flinched and tried to flatten herself against the wall. Val reached out and smoothed the girl's hair from her face before pushing Monet's hands away from her bandages. The girl slapped at Val's hands. Phaedra smiled as Val's raspy voice filled her office.

"Hey! Stop it, or I'll hit you my goddamned self. Phaedra's not even interested in you. Your mother was who she wanted all along. You're just some fucking pawn. Keep it up and I'll finish you myself." The sound of Val's voice filled Phaedra's office, and she settled in her chair.

"Alana put up with a lot to keep you safe. Bastards never let her live down what she was. Even now she suffers because of you. I know you can't hear me, but you understand what the fuck I'm saying, don't you? Don't you?" Val reared back as if to hit Monet, and the girl tucked her hands under her chin as she again turned her face against the wall.

Val spent a few more minutes with Monet, changing the dressing on her leg before she moved out of the line of sight. Phaedra smoothed her hair down and tried to look busy while she waited for Val to walk in.

"You wash your hands?" Phaedra muttered as Val walked in, working sanitizer into her hands.

"Now what do you think? You've been watching me on camera since you walked out."

"After all these years, you would think Alana was out of your system."

"Phaedra, she's busted up pretty bad. You wanted her here; now she's here. I pieced her back together, but it's gonna take a long while before she can move or do anything you want her to do. You should have sent me to get her. Your timetable is off now because you had to rush this."

"Sent you? You could barely keep your hands off her just now."

Val walked around the desk and leaned over Phaedra's chair.

"Who the fuck do you think you're talking to, huh? I'm not the architect of this shit; you are. Alana was fine where she was. I just cleaned up your mess, per usual."

"Get out of my way," Phaedra muttered as she gripped her chair and tried to stand.

"Sit the fuck down. I'm not finished. You thought this shit up. You planned this and for what?"

"Get..."

Phaedra tried again to stand. She put her hand on Val's shoulder to shove her away and saw the pain blossom in her face. Phaedra raised her hands, almost in a mock surrender.

Val swayed on her feet slightly, but she continued to grip the arms of Phaedra's chair. Val shook her head sharply to rid herself of the dizzy spell.

"Answer me because it wasn't about Julian Barlow. You two weren't even that thick."

"I was in his stable long before Alana was. Why are you still defending her after what she did," Phaedra hissed? "You waited out on the tarmac in the cold and rain for hours. She didn't even call."

"I told you to leave it alone, Phae. Alana was broken. She couldn't travel even if she had wanted to. Just leave it alone."

"Why, because it's her? I mean, what is it about her? She's phony, always has been. Trying to be prim and proper when she's nothing more than trash, no better than the rest of us. It's like putting lipstick on a pig."

Val let go of Phaedra's chair and fell sideways into the one closest to her. Phaedra reached for her, and Val knocked her hand out of the way. "You would know, wouldn't you?"

Phaedra took in a sharp breath and looked away.

"I know you don't mean that. I know I made you angry. I'm sorry. She just gets under my skin." Phaedra turned, seeing Val holding a handkerchief under her nose to stop the bleeding. Phaedra moved her chair closer, took the soaked cloth and replaced it with a handful of tissues.

"I'm sorry, Val. I didn't mean to."

"You never mean to, Phaedra. Christ, what's it gonna take? I married *you*. That should have been enough."

"But Alana..."

"Was happy in her life. Once I found out she was alive, hell I was happy for her. We weren't even a blip on her screen until you threw a grenade into her life. What the fuck did you *think* was going to happen? That thing with the necklace was a mind fuck. No one else knew that medallion belonged to the cop's twin brother. You had to know she'd expect us."

"She has to pay for..."

"What exactly? You keep saying she did something to hurt you, but you never say exactly what that was. Just 'She knows what she did.' That other shit was a job. She didn't plan it. You know it was all Barlow. After all this time Phaedra, why?"

"You can ask me that after what she did." Phaedra took the bloody Kleenex and handed Val another wad.

"Here we go. What did she do that was so awful, besides attempting to get you out of 'The Life'? She fought like hell to get us to one of the safehouses. There were people ready to get us someplace clean and quiet. Someplace other than a home where the male members of your family passed you around like a blunt."

"Was where I ended up really any better?"

"You *chose* to go back. You thought that Julian would accept you, welcome you home after you told him where we were. He didn't though. He just pawned you off on someone in Lisbon."

"Julian's blood is on her hands."

"A lot of blood is on Alana's hands, but if I can forgive her, why can't you?" Val said as she stood and walked away.

CHAPTER 18

The sun bounced off the snow in a vicious glare as Cass pulled up on the scene. In the light of day, there were still uniforms trudging back and forth, in and out of the woods. Cass closed his eyes and willed himself to go still. The feeling was the same. There was a distinct lack of Alana in the area. Cass leaned forward against his steering wheel. He felt Mark squeeze his shoulder.

"Thought you said she wasn't out here, man."

"She's not."

"Then why are we here? Levine is waiting for us at the Federal Building."

"There's something I need to see. I noticed it this morning. Alana isn't into wasted motion. Everything she does is deliberate, from washing dishes to making love. She's always right there in the present. Always focused on who and what is in front of her and around her. Alana and the kids loved the snow; they would trudge back and forth for hours. She taught them how to track animals and how to make snow angels and glyphs. She called them messages in the snow. There's one in the back yard under Gabe's window."

"What's it say?"

"Love."

"She never seemed to show it."

Cass turned in his seat. Mark held up a hand.

"I'm just saying."

Cass studied his friend for a long time.

"I lied to you and Myra about Gabe's birth." Cass took in a steadying breath that rushed through his teeth. "He wasn't born in a hospital in France. Alana's cesarean section was self-inflicted."

"You mean she…" Mark's mouth fell open.

"She was terrified that someone was going to take him from us." Cass shifted uneasily in his seat and gripped the steering wheel in both fists. "Alana used all the towels in the linen closet because she didn't want to make a mess. Had to kick the door in to get to her."

Mark put a hand on his shoulder and Cass shrugged him off.

"We didn't think we could get pregnant. She already had three miscarriages because Julian stomped…" Cass cleared his throat and looked over at his friend. "Monet was the only one that survived because she kept her a secret."

Mark moved to say something then put his head down.

Cass touched his friend's shoulder.

"Lydia thinks Alana trained soldiers, and maybe she did. All I know is that my children were safer than most because of it. If that's not love, then I don't know what is."

Cass threw his shoulder into his truck door and climbed out. At once, he was assaulted by the cacophony of sounds that always came to him at a crime scene.

The crackle and whine of the police chatter on walkie-talkies was overshadowed by the sound of men calling to each other and the buzz of choppers overhead. Cass shrugged deeper into his coat as he made his way over to the tents. The sheriff he'd seen the night before came out to meet them.

"Good morning, Mr. Garrett... Mark... Can't imagine how hard this must be coming back down here. You said something about wanting to look at the photos we took. We have them posted inside."

Mark shot a look at Cass as he followed the sheriff into the tent.

"In the light of day, we can piece together more of what happened to your wife, and I'm willing to concede that she may, and I say this with caution, she *may* have walked out of here alive." The sheriff pointed at the whiteboard that stood on the far side of the tent. Cass made his way through the crowd of men.

"Look, can you all head outside?" Mark yelled. "You're underfoot." Some of the men looked at the sheriff, and Mark moved forward. "Was that a look? While on scene I am in charge, and I'm telling you to move your asses outside."

As the men filed out, Cass moved closer to the board. A plastic bag with an orange evidence sticker caught his eye. He stepped closer to see the remnants of a shattered mug. He took in a sharp breath, then shook his head before turning to look at the whiteboards filled with pictures.

He took in the aerial photos of the woods and the area around the tree where he found Gabriel. Just as he thought, the snow had been trampled through, but there were close-ups of blood in the snow. Cass reached out to touch the photo then thought better of it. He glanced around at the other photos.

"We're still searching... We have surveillance tapes from the Wal-Mart Superstore where your wife was last seen getting into the truck with your son." The sheriff touched Cass' shoulder and pointed to the monitors.

Cass watched as Alana and Gabriel made their way to her truck. Alana turned her head to scan the area around her, and Cassi felt his heart thud sickly in his chest. She carefully placed their son in and fixed the seatbelt over him.

"She always that careful with him?" the sheriff whispered to Mark.

"Since the day he was born." Cass blinked back tears, then noticed the Hummer pulling out behind Alana. "Wait a minute. Run that back."

The tech that was sitting at the computer complied, and Cass' back straightened. "Look at the plates. That's no ordinary truck; that's Fed issued."

"We found it out at the airport. Stolen from a shop not too far from here."

"Was my wife's blood in the trunk?"

"Yeah."

Cass turned on the sheriff. "Is somebody out at the airport?"

"Surveillance picked up two men loading what amounted to a footlocker onto a private jet."

"Heading where? Somebody has to have the flight manifest."

The sheriff looked over at Mark for help then dropped his shoulders. "Unknown."

Cass glanced back over his shoulder at the pictures on the board, and one caught his eye. He pulled it off the board and studied it. "You knew they were coming for you, didn't you?"

Mark moved closer. "What? Cass, you saying she knew this would happen?"

"Alana told me herself, but I wasn't listening. I didn't want to hear her, but she knew. Told me once that she would do what she had to, and she knew I would too."

"Cass, you're not making sense."

"I went to the center this morning. I talked to some of the girls there. They said there was one girl that was there and then gone. She fit the description I gave Myra. They told me her name was Stacey."

"Was?"

"Vice found her body stuffed in a trash chute in a housing project in Robey."

"Why didn't Alana call us and tell us her suspicions?"

"Mark, this is Alana we're talking about. Since when has she ever trusted the police?"

Mark sighed and shook his head slowly. "Truth. I spoke with Megan. She's part of the K-9 Unit... one of Alana's success stories. She fell apart. I asked her if she knew anything but got nada. She ain't one for a whole lot of talking either. But you said Alana was waiting?"

Cass turned to Mark and pressed the picture into his hands.

"It's what she's been waiting for. She tried to tell me, but I wouldn't listen, wouldn't allow her to tell me all of it. I didn't understand. She knew they would never let her live in peace. But they were her handlers. She made it seem like they might have even loved her." He walked toward the tent entrance with Mark on his heels.

"Who are "they"? Cass, wait. Where are you going?" Mark looked down at the photo and stopped in his tracks. Although the snow was churned up, obliterating some of the letters, Mark could make out the word Alana had formed with her footsteps: *Isla*.

CHAPTER 19

Cass walked into the Federal building with Mark, and they were immediately escorted upstairs. Mark looked around like a tourist while He searched the room for Levine. Cass took in a deep, shuddery breath as the familiarity of the place called to him from all sides. The place was deserted, but it still had that cold, sterile, agitated feel to it, as if the world were on the brink and this room, the 'War Room' as they called it, was waiting for the countdown to Doomsday.

"So, this is where you were all those years," Mark murmured as he continued to take in the place.

Cass glanced over at his old friend.

"You know I understood why you left the force, Cass."

"Lydia seems to think the guys lost all respect for me when I made my move."

"None were brave enough to say it to my face. Besides, half of them wanted to *be* you. They didn't lose respect; they were jealous because you always seemed to land in the catbird seat. Nobody before or since caught a case like Alana's. You were a legend. She bordered on being a myth. The governor is still waiting for you to become Maryland's top cop. Hell, I'm just keeping the seat warm. I'd step down if you came back. Besides, I never lost respect. I saw what almost losing her did to you."

Cass took in a deep breath and looked away. The decision had been an easy one. The memory was so clear in his mind. Alana was sitting in Lydia's rocking chair with Monet curled up against her. Broken and bloody, Alana still had that regal look to her.

When she spilled out of the chair into his arms asking for forever, every decision after that became easy. Whatever it took to be near her, he would do it. "Patrick Cohn was the one that suggested I take a job here. He was there that night at the hospital when I brought her in."

"So was I, Cass. Took me and four other people to talk you into putting her down on the gurney. You never left her side—not even in the morgue," Mark said.

Cass closed his eyes against the memory and shook away the thoughts. He was okay until she reached out and touched the bastard's face. Julian had already caused her enough pain. When he gathered her back into his arms, Cass swore an oath that Alana would never know another second of pain. He shook his head sharply to rid himself of the memory and looked over at Mark.

"Patrick Cohn—Teacher, as everyone called him—knew that once Alana was well enough to sit up in a chair they had every intention of interrogating her until they had every connection, every network, every... Remember the legal pads Alana wrote on in our interrogation room back in Shadow Bay?" Cass turned to look at Mark once more.

"Saw pictures of them once I was released from the hospital. I never saw them with my own eyes," Mark said as he rubbed at the old bullet wound in his thigh. "The way I hear it, those things became the Holy Grail."

"Years of investigative work. She laid out plans and networks that were so intricate, so subtle, that on the outside it all looked innocent. Blood diamonds, conflict minerals, generations of tribes of people locked in a battle over stones like the ones Alana used as jacks. She knew about politicians that were involved in trafficking everything from humans to guns, the death toll, the lives that were saved or ruined depending on what side of the law you were on. She was plutonium. Men tried to use her up, but they also underestimated her. After all, what could a young temp worker for a local bank filled with welfare moms and blue-haired old ladies know? All of it rested on her shoulders and her talent. And it would have gone on until she died." Cass glanced at his old desk.

"Alana was the perfect work horse, Mark. Dependable, always got the job done. To this day, her mouth gets watery like she's going to vomit if someone tells her they appreciate her. Appreciate what exactly? That she did her little dance? That she agonized over every member of her team that never made it back? Julian got the butter from the duck every single time she went out on a job. He had no intentions of stopping. Two, three jobs in a night. Even here, it wasn't until they found out that she knew where the bodies in this agency were buried that they started easing up on the assignments."

"You're right, Cass. She made and ruined a lot of careers around here. Her commendations rivaled some of the lifers in this building," Levine said.

Cass and Mark turned to see Levine standing just outside one of the interrogation rooms.

"Alana was my one human credential into this place. Which was laughable because her credit here was only borrowed. If she ever stopped dancing, she knew there would be consequences. Teacher was the only one who thought I could be objective enough to help them root out all the leads she'd given us. But at first, it was obvious no one wanted either one of us here."

CHAPTER 20

Levine held the door as both men walked inside and took a seat at the long conference table.

"Where is everybody? It looks like a ghost town out there," Mark said.

"Still early, morning roll call and the usual monthly staff meetings," Levine said looking at Mark. Then Levine turned and looked at Cass. "Most, if not all, of our teams are still out on scene or looking into things for you."

Cass's gaze was trained on the wall in the far corner of the room.

Levine followed his gaze. "Teacher referred to that corner as Alana's office. She rarely chose a chair. Teacher said she would come in and wedge herself in that area over there," Levine said as he continued to stare at the corner.

"It was easier for her to see the entire room," Cass said softly. "Used to sit right beside her."

Levine cleared his throat, and Cass looked around at him.

"Do you have any idea who would want to hurt Alana or take Monet?"

Mark sat up in his chair. "Wait a minute. I thought she was away at college. You're telling me Mo's involved?"

Cass glanced over at Mark. Some private message passed between them, and Mark settled back in his chair.

"Devil will have his due," Cass said softly.

Both men stared at Cass whose gaze drifted back to the corner.

"Something Alana said to me. Nature of the beast...necessary evil. It was all the same to Alana. She understood things that... I mean, sure she made careers and put a lot of bad people away and served her time, but she always knew. Her understanding of how the real world worked was always much clearer than anything most people were reared to believe."

Mark reached out and put his hand on Cass' arm. "Cass, you're not making sense."

Cass took in a painfully deep breath. "It was why she was up at all hours of the night, searching the dark. Alana knew that one day someone would find her and make her pay for talking to us... to me. It's what she was trying to tell me, and I wouldn't hear her," he said softly.

Cass scrubbed the space between his eyebrows with the heel of his hand. "I brought her to this," he said finally.

"To say Alana had enemies would be an understatement. Her Holy Grail alone recovered millions... billions of dollars globally. She even destabilized a couple of regions with what she knew. It wasn't all paintings and gemstones like everybody thought. It was the people she knew, the people who knew her." Cass looked up at Levine.

"Alana gave Teacher and the others what they asked for, but it didn't cover even half of what she knew. It's why they kept calling her in. Kept asking her to perform her talents, just on a different level. She was better than any agent at getting into places no one else could."

"Are you saying...?"

Cass waved his hand to silence him. "We used her, Mark. Only then we called it 'consulting'. It was all for the cause, but Alana was the only one paying."

"Now, Cass, wait a minute."

Cass palmed at his eye, batting away tears. "You know something? She admitted to me that she chose to go to prison after a few years, just so that she could rest."

"She consented. No one ever forced her." Levine looked down at the files in front of him. "Teacher would never..."

Something between a laugh and a sob leapt from Cass's throat. "Julian probably said the same thing."

"Cass, don't." Mark reached for his arm, and Cass pulled away.

"Past is present. Present is past. Alana trained our children to protect themselves until one or both of us came for them. Alana did it because she loved them... loved me. She did it because she knew that as an extension of her they would--we would--all be targets. We were trying for another baby. No, I wanted another baby, and Alana kept putting it off. Last night was proof of why she wanted to wait."

"Cass, I know she did things, things she thought she had to do to protect Monet. But there's no all-seeing dark force that compels people. Some of that stuff thrilled her. It had to. I mean, come on, Cass. She had what amounted to a Crown Royal bag filled with gemstones worth millions of dollars. You think maybe you're not completely objective here?" Mark asked.

Cass turned to face Mark. "You're wondering if I have a blind spot where Alana's concerned. Maybe you think that my moral compass is beyond screwed."

"Cass, I didn't mean to sound..."

Cass sat back in his chair and smiled at Mark. "Teacher didn't bring me on board because my moral compass was off. Teacher brought me on because Alana didn't have one. I understood that she didn't need one. All she knew how to do was survive, and until you've lived like that you really can't say what you will or won't do. None of us can," he said.

Cass turned back to Levine. "Who is Isla?" Reaching into his coat pocket, he pulled out the photograph of Alana's footprints in the snow. "Alana made this glyph in the snow while she was hiding our son. That message was for me. She's mentioned two people to me in the past, Knox and Isla. Who are they?"

* * *

"Harvey Knox was Teacher's first partner. They came up in MI5. Harvey was with the Mossad, the Israeli military, for years before he joined the agency. You talk about people being myths. This man succeeded," Levine said as he wiped at the sweat on his brow before rolling up his sleeves.

"And Isla?" Cass urged.

"Cass, we are getting into denied territory. Ever wonder why Alana got the golden parachute? Harvey Knox and Isla Ado put a bug in the ear of someone in the Justice Department; a large bug, with lots of legs and progeny.

"The information they had could have toppled governments, even ours. Alana wasn't supposed to see a day of prison. You're right; Alana *agreed* to go, maybe to rest, but also to spare Knox and Isla. The give and take between the three of them made absolutely no sense, but it scared a lot of people. Powerful people." The color drained from Levine's face as he spoke.

"Alana said they were her handlers when she was a child. Something about Dominic Mandylor bringing her to them to train," Cass said as he looked around the table at both men. "It's all I have, but it's a place to begin."

CHAPTER 21

Val watched from the door as Monet cradled Alana on her lap. Val took a drag from the cigarillo she had wedged between her fingers. The smoke that billowed softly around her had the distinct smell of vanilla, with a hint of marijuana to it. It took everything in Val not to walk over and yank the girl out of the bed by her hair.

It was Monet's fault that Alana had been found. Vincent was easy to buy. All the girl had to do was listen to her mother, go to school and remain in her rooms, but her brain went to her ass and now they were all waiting for Alana to recover and get back to the business of dying in the way Phaedra was accustomed to: *Humiliate them first and watch them suffer.* That was Phaedra's mantra.

There wasn't much time. After their last fight and their last make-up session, Phaedra had agreed to release Monet. The moratorium on Phaedra's mercy was about as fickle as the moon. It waxed and waned according to her moods.

Val wanted to be the one to return Monet to the States, but the thought of leaving Alana alone with Phaedra rooted Val in place. Val tilted her head as she continued to watch Monet dote over her mother.

Keeping Alana heavily sedated while she healed was the only way to keep her from causing any more damage, but in reality, it was another way to keep Phaedra in the wings. The minute Alana opened her eyes, the minute she sat up and threw her legs over the side of the bed, the nightmare would begin again.

Val glanced over her shoulder to see her younger brother, Brian, standing in the shadows.

"Do you have the cop's address?" she asked softly as she took another drag from her cigarillo.

"Yes."

"Make sure you leave her exactly where I tell you. Don't go ringing doorbells and shit. Get her there and get gone. Not another scratch on her, you hear me. If I find out she's been touched... anybody tries to mess with that child, they won't have themselves to worry about. Let them know, Brian. I kill families first."

Brian moved to step into the room, and Val held up her hand. "Wait."

Val walked slowly over to the bed. Monet wrapped a possessive arm around her mother.

"My father taught me this trick. He called it a lesson, a reminder of what would happen if I ever developed a brain and decided to tell. Remember, Brian? Dad was always good at teaching us a lesson after using us as his own personal toilet. Most, if not all, of my beatings turned into rapes. How about yours, Bri? You don't have to answer. I remember the screams." Val took another pull from her cigarillo and blew on the tip until it turned a malevolent orange. Monet moved her arm just enough for Val to move closer.

"You see, that is the difference between you two. Your mother would have taken the burns for you," Val said before she sat down on the side of the bed. "Took the burns for me once, did you know that? Course not, you weren't even here yet."

Val tucked the cigarillo holder between her teeth then pulled back the sheet enough to lift Alana's left hand onto her lap. Val turned Alana's arm so that two small burn scars the size of quarters stared back at her. Val's eyes welled with tears. She ran her thumb over the scars.

"Your mother played a game of strip poker with my father. Only he didn't want her naked. He wanted her to scream. My father fed off screams. Mine, my kid brother's, the neighbor's kid. It egged him on. Your mother took these burns for me and far worse. Never understood why... could never figure out why. She knew he was going to kill us that night to shut us up... just like all the others. She was there trying to get us out that night, but he came home. He was the youth pastor at our church. Everybody loved him. I didn't even see the knife, but Alana did and ended up trying to hold her arm together till we could get her some help. William…. Whispers took care of my father in the end. And Alana made us a family. Got some of us to safety, but never herself. Just kept coming back for us. Just one more trip and I'll go. She used to say that all the time."

Val ran her thumb over the old knife wound that screamed down Alana's arm. Monet moved, and Val shot the girl a look that made her cringe back in the corner while trying feebly to pull her mother with her. Val loosened the wedding rings on Alana's hand, then pulled them off and shook them in her tiny fist like dice, before she looked at them.

"I know you can't hear me, Monet. You're too scared to understand anything, even if I were to use sign language. The cop loves your mother. If he's smart, he'll just let this run its course. If not, you and your brother will end up just like me and Brian over there. Only there won't be anybody to stand in the gap for you."

Monet drew her hand back to slap Val. Brian stepped forward. Val caught the girl's hand and pried it open. She folded the rings into Monet's hand.

"Get her out of here." Val muttered through gritted teeth as she pulled Alana over onto her lap.

Brian dragged Monet from the bed and out the door.

When they were alone, Val clutched Alana to her chest and simply sat there. "Never had a chance to thank you for saving our lives, Alana."

Val gently eased her back down against the pillows, smoothing the hair back from her face. She closed her own eyes against the tears that burned in them.

"She's safe, Alana. You hear me? I sent her home with your rings. Maybe if he sees them, maybe it will be enough. You wanted to be dead to the world once. Now you are."

Val traced the curve of Alana's cheek with her thumb. She caught herself leaning forward to kiss Alana, but she stopped. Instead, she took another pull from her cigarillo and busied herself with fixing the blankets around Alana.

"I kept my word. Now you gotta come through. You listening to me?"

* * *

Cass poured over the photos that covered his kitchen table. The silence in the house was deafening. At least with Alana there he could feel her moving through the place. There was a lack of sound to her, but the silence was somehow filled with her.

Gabe napped on the chair next to him, wrapped in his mother's shawl. Cass patted his son's back, and he woke up.

"Hey bud, you wanna go sit in Mom's chair in the living room?"

Gabe buried his head in Cass's side before he hopped down from the chair.

Cass stood in the doorway long enough to see Gabe climb into the ornate rocking chair Cass had made for Alana. Whiskey settled on the floor in front of Gabe and put his head down on his paws.

Once his son was out of the room, Cass felt his composure slip as he examined the box in front of him. Gabe had been in Alana's library most of the day. When Myra left to go home, he emerged holding a jigsaw puzzle box. Instead of taking a seat at the table, he came straight to Cass.

"Hey bud, what's in there."

"Mommy's things." Cass sat Gabe on his lap and took the box.

"She told me to give this to you if she was ever late coming home."

"She say anything else?" Cass put the box down on the table and covered it with his hand.

"Mommy's never late." Gabe's eyes filled with tears, and he shook his head.

At that, Cass clutched him to his chest.

He shuddered inwardly as he turned his attention back to the puzzle box on the table.

Cass smoothed his hand over the brightly colored lid touting hours of fun with this puzzle of European tourist attractions.

He took in a breath and pulled off the lid.

CHAPTER 22

Levine and his men had cleared out before sunrise, leaving just Cass and Gabriel in the house. Cass had given up trying to convince his son to head back to school. In truth, he was nervous to have Gabe more than a few feet from him. But Cass also needed time to think, time to plan, and looking at his son with dark circles around his eyes and the grief that seemed to cover the little boy like a wet blanket was more than he could stand. He caught a glimpse of his cell phone jittering across the table and grabbed it.

"Speak."

"Hey man, me and Myra are on our way back over. You gotta know Gabe isn't going to take it well; you are leaving him."

Cass looked across the kitchen to see Gabriel's skateboard sitting silently in the corner.

"You're wrong about that. I gave him his skateboard early. We sanded it down and put on the grips. He already knows I'm going after his mother and sister. He wants me to"

"Cass, what if..."

"Don't even say it, Mark. I know she's not."

"You have a blind spot where she's concerned."

"Maybe I do. All I know is my son needs his mother."

"And what do you need?"

"Doesn't matter now. My son needs his family, the family me and Alana made."

"Sounds more like you're talking about yourself. What if the life you're fighting for never existed? I'm just saying..."

"Don't. I'm not delusional. There are things about Alana that even I don't understand after all these years. I watched Monet detach from the world while her mother was in prison. For weeks she was like a living doll. I see the same thing right now in Gabe. But then Alana came home, and it was like I could breathe again; we both could. The world had color. My children love me, but they *need* her.

Alana loved...loves…me and our children. That is a fact. Gabe said something along those lines the other day. Alana wasn't just careful with Gabe, she was careful with all of us, as though on some level she didn't think she deserved us. I know that Alana was broken in ways that even I couldn't fix, but she stayed with me, allowing me to build a world, a life, for her away from the blood and the pain."

Mark was quiet for a long time. "So when do you leave?"

"Levine is reaching out to some thumbtacks and assembling a team."

"Where will you look? I mean, this Harvey Knox, is that even his real name?"

"Probably not, but we're going with it. "

Cass put the lid back on the puzzle box and studied the old man in the photos spread across the table. The man reminded Cass of somebody's grandfather. Harvey's shoulders were bowed in toward his chest, and his back was curved with arthritis. For all the frailty the man seemed to possess, his eyes never changed. There was a cruelty to them, a defiance that silently telegraphed, *Yes, I did it, and I'm not sorry*.

"Dad!" Gabriel screamed.

Cass rose to his feet.

"Cass, what's wrong? Cass?" Mark yelled into the phone.

"I think Gabe's having another nightmare. He keeps screaming for Alana."

"He ain't calling Alana though."

Cass moved around the table and headed for the living room.

"Daddy!"

Gabe's voice emanated from outside. Through the open front door, he saw his son in his pajamas out in the snow holding Monet. Cass dropped the phone and ran outside.

* * *

Levine paced back and forth in front of the examination room at the ER. Cass sat in the chair just outside the door with Gabe on his lap with his face pressed into Cass's shoulder. "We had men on you, Cass. I don't get it."

"You've been compromised."

Levine turned toward Cass to protest, but then he stopped and nodded. "Knox has been known to short circuit investigations."

Just then, the doctor came out, and Cass stood, passing Gabe off to Myra.

"Your daughter is fine, all things considered. She's in shock. It appears that..."

Rather than let the doctor finish, Cass reached out and grabbed the man's arm to lead him away from Myra and Gabe. "Start over."

"Well, it appears that your daughter has been shot. The wound is closing nicely. Someone got her help, cleaned her up. I've only seen that kind of stitchery in the OR. Other than that, there's not a scratch on her. She's a little dehydrated, but other than that she's fine."

"Was she..."

The doctor rested his hand on Cass's shoulder. "There's no evidence of that, thank God. But we couldn't get any information out of her. She just keeps trying to get out of the bed, so we sedated her."

"She needs to talk to us, doctor."

"She needs rest more than anything," the doctor urged.

"Can I see her?"

"Of course. I don't think it's wise to take your son in there, though."

Both men looked back at Gabe as he squirmed in Myra's arms. Cass shrugged his shoulders. "He's the one that found her, but I hear you. I wasn't planning on taking him in there. He came unglued when he found her. Wouldn't let anyone come near her at first. Kept begging me to get them to the panic room."

Cass walked over to the door and pushed his way in. The nurses were adjusting a bag of clear fluid on an IV pole. Cass moved over to the bed fully expecting to see Monet asleep. Instead, she was looking at him with tears leaking from her eyes.

"Hey, baby girl." Cass pressed a kiss to her forehead and slipped her hair behind her ears. She sat up in his arms, and he simply held her trembling body. Monet jerked away from him. Only then did he notice that one of her hands was balled into a fist. "You're safe, honey. I'm right here. Did they break her hand?" He looked back at one of the nurses.

Both women shook their heads and moved closer. Cass smoothed his hand over her fist, and Monet grabbed his hand and poured the rings into it. At once her hands began to flutter in front of her. Mark walked in carrying Gabriel.

"Cass, what's she saying?" he whispered.

"See, Dad, I told you."

Cass turned to see Gabe wriggle his way out of Mark's grasp.

"Cass...what's she saying?" Mark moved into the room with Myra on his heels.

"Mom's hurt. She couldn't wake her up." Gabe said as he climbed on the bed. "Mo didn't want to leave. Some lady made her leave."

A private looked passed between Mark and Cass as Gabe took the medallion from around his neck and placed it over Monet's head.

"Who made her leave, Gabe." Cass smoothed a hand over Gabe's back. "Mo talk to me. Who made you leave?"

Monet gripped Cass by the arm and tried to sit up as she mouthed the words twice before she passed out. Gabe wrapped one arm around her and reached for Cass.

"Cass, man, you gotta give me something to work from. Who has Alana? Where is she?"

Cass swallowed against the chunk of his heart crowding his throat before he spoke.

"France." The words stuck in his throat. "Skeleton Woman has her."

Gabe curled up next to Monet as his eyes flooded with tears. He hid his face in Monet's arm and sobbed.

"You gotta find her Dad."

CHAPTER 23

Harvey Knox tilted his face to the early morning sunlight. He let his eyes slip shut as the smell of croissants and freshly brewed coffee beckoned him to one of his usual haunts.

Gun oil and American sweat were a strange addition to the sights, sounds, and smells that he was used to experiencing near his home in France. The Americans had been onto him for several weeks. Knox allowed them to trail him around Greece and Italy as he searched for Alana. As he took his first sip of coffee, he thought about the African American man who seemed to be at the helm.

Finding out about Cassiel Garrett was simple enough. Knox had been away from the agency for years, but his own connections still squawked when he did. More than once, Knox considered walking right up and asking him where Alana was, but Knox already knew the answer.

The underground networks crackled and hummed with the knowledge that Alana Symone was missing and believed to be dead. Knox took in a cleansing breath and sat his cup down. He tapped the earpiece wedged in his ear.

"Welcome to Paris, gentlemen. This message is for the American, Cassiel Garrett. I should be home later this evening. Don't bother trying to follow me. You already know where I live. Come alone or I'm in the wind. I'll tell you what I know."

* * *

The villa reminded Cass of a picture postcard. Everything about the place seemed perfectly sculpted to lure tourists or celebrities to some late-night dinner party, instead of being the home of a federal agent that had fallen from grace.

"Come in, Garrett. Don't be shy."

Cass pulled his gun and walked inside. He checked to make sure the area was secure before moving into a galley-style kitchen. A wooden ceiling fan circulated the air around them, diffusing the scent of gardenias throughout the room. The walls in the hallway were covered in jigsaw puzzles that had been glued together. He paused to take in some of the Great European Landmarks and Museums that covered the walls and even the ceiling. The faint light from the kitchen caught on the crazy quilt of lines each piece made in the final picture. He moved a little further, and he noticed a room off to his left with a floor to ceiling bookshelf filled with books. Cass finally made his way into the kitchen.

The old man was standing at the stove stirring a sauce in a large grey pot. Knox carefully sat the wooden spoon aside and turned to Cass with his hands held out. The white, button-down shirt the man wore was covered with an even whiter apron. The charcoal grey slacks and slippers completed the man's look. Knox stuck two fingers in the cuff of one sleeve and then the other.

"Nothing up my sleeves. Put away your gun, Garrett. There's no one here to harm you-just a very tired old man,"

Knox shuffled over to the table. His white hair was pulled back in a ponytail. He placed both hands on the table to steady himself as he lowered into the chair, then extended his hand to the empty seat.

Cass scanned the area once more before he lowered his gun. "You knew we were following you. So why the cloak and dagger?"

"Needed some time to think, so I let you do a little sightseeing."

"My wife is missing. I don't have time to sightsee. If you took her, if you paid somebody to take my wife..."

"I'd never be that cruel." The old man tilted his head and smiled, yet it never quite reached his eyes.

"Why not, you were before."

His grizzled features hardened into a smirk that made Cass's skin crawl.

"I don't have to justify anything I've done, to you."

"Our son is a walking wound. His sister is no better. I don't have time to verbally spar with you."

"She walked away from you…"

"No, she didn't. She was *taken* from me."

The old man settled back in his chair and reached for the crystal snifter on the table. He swirled the amber liquid inside before taking a sip. "Have some?"

"My wife." Cass felt his muscles tighten in his arms as his hands involuntarily closed into a fist.

Harvey took another sip, but his eyes never left Cass's. In fact, the more Cass watched him, the more the casual, yet deliberate and measured way the man moved seemed familiar.

"How'd you meet her." Knox tilted his head as if to acknowledge some private question.

"A bank back in Shadow Bay, Maryland. She saved my life."

"She does that a lot, does she? Save your life, I mean. She took a bullet or two for you…they ate through her like starved rats to get to you. Please, sit down, Mr. Garrett."

Knox extended his pale gnarled, hand to the chair across from him again.

"Sit or stand, Garrett, makes no difference to me. But I should think you would be tired of all these dead ends."

Cass studied the old man across the table. "Why...?"

"Like I said. I needed time to think. You wanted to search for Alana, and I was helping do that very thing. It was why you were in Athens, no? Some federal snitch sighted Alana at a party or some such? All those leads were planted."

"How do you know."

"Alana isn't seen unless she wants to be. More likely she's incapacitated."

Cass searched the surface of the table as tears beveled his view. He blinked and shook his head sharply.

"She was hurt. I don't know how badly. There was blood in the snow."

Cass fell into the chair across from the old man and searched the tablecloth once more. "She *is* alive. I know it,"

Harvey's eyes lit up as a brilliant smile warmed his craggy features. "You can still feel her. That's good. If you can still feel that pull inside of you then that's very good. Follow that."

"Who are you? I mean really, *who are you*? Did you take my wife?"

"Of course not. I'd never frighten her or her little girl like that. I loved her."

"Yeah, you loved her enough to shoot her up with enough drugs to almost kill her. You loved her enough to burn away her fingerprints." Cass choked on the last few words as he sat his gun on the table.

"I was a better father to Chuisle"

"Her *name* is Alana."

"Chuisle means sweetheart."

"I don't give a damn what it means, where is my wife?"

"I gave her a gift that may not have made sense to you, but it spared her time and time again just as it spared Isla."

"And where is Isla? Who is she to Alana?"

"She goes by Alana now. Isla would say it was a good name."

"Then where is she? Where's Isla?"

The old man winced as tears filled his muddy brown eyes. He downed the cognac, poured another, then tipped a casual salute to an empty chair that held a shawl that looked a lot like Alana's.

"My Isla is dead."

The pain in Cass' chest made it harder to breathe. The only reason he came alone was because of the prospect of speaking to Isla.

"She came to visit Alana while she was in prison, did Alana tell you? We stared at our beautiful little girl encased in glass like a jewel."

"Alana is not your child. No parent would do what you did."

"Actually, she is. Isla was pregnant when I left her in Sierra Leone. Neither of us knew at the time. Twins actually. She miscarried the boy crossing the desert." Knox rested his elbows on the table as he hugged his arms. "Alana survived just like always."

CHAPTER 24

"Your children are alive because of what she... what *I* taught Alana. She brought him to us when he was an infant. Did you know that?"

"Impossible." Cass shook his head. "Alana would never put our son in harm's way"

Knox shook his head and smiled. "Isla showed her how to steal, honed Alana's innate gift to fade into the scenery, to hide in plain sight. Made her study any and everything. You'd think she was building an old-world courtesan, but Isla was fashioning something worse."

"You said Alana brought my son to see the two of you."

"Yes, she did. At any given time, Alana was surrounded by millions of dollars, but her masterpiece, her treasures were her children. They were her victory."

Cass grabbed the bottle of cognac and the empty snifter sitting on his side of the table. He tried not to notice the way Knox stared at him.

"Where is my wife, Knox?"

"You're wondering how you fit into her victory."

"I know where I am in her victory, as you call it. Alana took two cop killer rounds for me. I went to that prison every week and watched her die a little each time I saw her. Went there once and saw her covered in bruises and scratches she refused to explain." Cass downed the liquid and set his glass on the table.

"Look, this is pointless. It's obvious you know something, or think you do. Just tell me so that I can be on my way."

"Did you know they came to her nightly while she was in prison? Julian had enemies all over the place. People that he paid and betrayed. Somebody had to pay the freight, and with Julian dead who was left? Who paid the freight?" the man took a sip from his glass then sat it down neatly and turned it in a circle on the tablecloth. Cass sat back in the chair and stared at the man.

"She did it to protect you. If she didn't see you, then she wouldn't have to lie. If she didn't know where you were, she didn't have to worry that they did. Always thinking three and four steps ahead, for herself and the people around her."

"I never gave Alana a chance to tell me anything. I didn't want her to think she had to apologize for her existence. When she married me I wanted her to know she was *with* me. I wanted her to know she was safe and loved, and I was... am her husband. I'm supposed to protect her."

"And that was how I saw my Isla. I wanted her to be safe and loved. I see myself in you."

"Please, we are nothing alike, Knox. I didn't subject Alana to acid washes to burn away her identity."

"Still beating that dead horse. The acid wash was Isla's idea. It was the only way she could think of to protect her. I tried to lessen the pain, and I gave her too much heroin. Thankfully, Alana didn't develop a taste for the stuff."

"No, you just stopped her heart. You think that makes what you did okay?"

"Was it any different for you?"

"I don't know what you're talking about."

"Of course, you do, Cassiel; you must. Alana had a talent that couldn't be wasted. Knowledge that made or broke careers. The federal government found a new use for her, but you found an even better one. Didn't you?"

"It's not the same. It wasn't the same. Alana suggested it."

"She suggested it to spare you. And how is your business doing? Securities? Consulting? Just a little to get that woodworking business off the ground. Who better to test drive a new security system than a known jewel thief? You were legit, but you were no better than Julian."

Cass rose to his feet. "That is not..."

"What, true? How long did she have to sit in those interrogation rooms? How long did she have to work for the agency to buy her true freedom? Is there such a thing? Put away your pride. Isla did the same thing for me. Why else do you think I'm sitting here in a villa like a small country squire?"

Cass spilled back into the chair and stared at the table.

"You gave up your career in local law enforcement to follow her, didn't you?"

Cass nodded slowly. "I watched her do things that to this day I can't explain. I watched her get into places that nobody, I mean nobody, could get into. She commanded teams of people, mine included. We never lost a man; do you hear me? Not even once. She caught everything. Even the slightest thing, stuff I didn't even pick up on, and I have years on the force." Cass said as he stared at the bottom of his shot glass. "We used her. *I* used... her. But I gave up my career, my life, to follow her."

The old man simply shook his head and smiled. "Never evened out did it? Somehow Alana always seemed to pay more—was called on to sacrifice more. Inside and out. What did they call it, serving justice? Taking one for the cause?"

Cass downed another shot of cognac before he nodded.

"I did the same thing—gave it all up for Isla. My assignment was to track her down and exterminate her. She knew far too much about far too many people. People she'd stolen a lot of things from; information she brokered. When I caught up to her, Isla gave me the option. Made me hold the gun to her head. What was the bigger act of cruelty, Cassiel?

Letting Isla die without knowing what it was like to be loved, or killing her because it was my assignment?" The old man splashed some cognac in his empty snifter and downed it.

"I could see what the heists were doing to Alana. She would come to me broken and bloody. She'd break into my apartment. I think it was the only place she felt reasonably safe, and even that came at a price. I thought, if Alana let me in, that I could fix it. I would make her safe. At first, I was using her to get what I wanted. I never expected to fall in love with her. Once I did..." Cass shrugged.

"The rest fell away?" the old man continued for Cass.

Cass rubbed his temples suddenly exhausted from the man's confession. At long last, Cass had someone who understood.

"People wax and wane and pontificate about how they don't believe in a necessary evil. They talk about what they will and won't do. They've never had to make the awful decision as to which child will live or die. My Isla did."

The old man glanced out the window at the garden.

"Cassiel, ordinary people can't fathom eating from rubbish bins or allowing men to barter them like so much chattel. Isla and Alana were years apart but cut from the same bolt of cloth. The Shoah…the unspeakable they endured. If we are lucky there is only one tragedy. For people like Isla and Alana, there are many. Ordinary people live in their perfect little houses thinking they understand the world. They don't care or are too scared to know the truth. Sometimes evil prevails." Knox said as he reached over and turned off the stove.

"Alana understood that, lived it. She saved I don't know how many young girls from a lifetime in the skin trade." Cass said.

Knox reached across the table and gripped Cass' hand.

"There are those that think Alana and Isla did heinous things for the thrill of it. Some thought Alana and Isla were monsters."

"None of this leads me to my wife."

Cass moved his hand away as he stuck his gun back in the shoulder holster and fixed his jacket.

Harvey stood and shuffled around the table.

"It's why she gave them to you, the children I mean. Did she leave you something? Papers or offshore accounts? Maybe even a passport to open a hole in the world that you and your children could step through?" Harvey nodded and sat back with a satisfied smile. "She's put it in something insignificant. Hiding in plain sight."

Cass reached for his coat then smoothed it back into place.

"Again, none of this leads to Alana."

Cass pulled away from the old man and headed for the door.

"Phaedra Khalid and Valerie Banks resurfaced in Europe a few weeks after Alana went missing. They grew up with Alana. Both seemed to hate her enough to want her death then.

"Have you asked them?" Cass glanced over his shoulder.

In the twilight the cataract in the old man's left eye appeared almost white.

"Anyone that asks dies."

CHAPTER 25

Val took a deep drag from the cigarillo in her left hand. As she held her breath and waited for the buzz to wrap around her, she looked around her bedroom.

The room had a decidedly masculine look with all dark furniture and neutral highlights. A bar sat on one side of the suite while a massive library covered the other three walls.

Val smiled as she took in the stereo directly across from her bed and nodded at her decision years ago not to put a television there. There was no need to watch the news anymore. Nothing else mattered once Whispers and Phaedra finally half walked, half carried Val to the jet.

Alana wasn't coming, so the world stopped. Instead, Val entombed herself in her room and waited for the cancer to spread, hoping it would finish her at last. But then the word came that Alana was alive. Only with proof-of-life photos did Val even bother to sit up on the side of the bed that Alana was currently sleeping in.

As Val healed, Phaedra went back to business as usual, planning and revising ways to make Alana pay a debt she didn't owe.

Val let the marijuana seep into her veins as she leaned back in her recliner, draping her legs over one arm. She settled down far enough for Alana to fill her view. Val straightened the buttercream sheet that pooled around Alana's thigh before she traced her fingers over the cast on her ankle which was propped up on a pillow.

The injuries were slow to heal, but it was happening, and with each passing week the dread in Val's gut grew. She'd taken to having her chemotherapy treatments in the room in the event Alana woke up. Val even dressed in the room, always with a view of Alana from the mirrors in the walk-in closet.

"The Louvre Museum here in France. The Guggenheim in New York, but Venice is closer. Winter Palace, Museum Island in Germany, British Museum. The Book of Kells in Ireland. The list goes on. Some house art, while others house gems. Private collectors are just as formidable."

The disconnected sound of Alana's voice could have been coming from anywhere in the room or even from thousands of miles away on a phone. The effect was the same. Every nerve in Val's body converged in a thunderclap, making her flinch.

Alana's green eyes shifted slowly over her face. She reached over and touched Val's small foot which was encased in a blinding white sweat sock. Val ran her hand over the black outdoor winter cap that covered her head.

"Is that where The Splinter of Heaven is? Is it housed in one of those places?"

Alana moved to sit up, and Val was on her feet stubbing out her cigarillo. She inched her back against the pillows, relishing the feel of Alana's nakedness under the pale blue nightgown Val had purchased in the weeks before her abduction. Once she was settled, Alana patted the side of Val's face.

"Could be any one of those places or many others I would hide it in if I had it, which I don't"

"Alana, come on,"

"Have I ever lied to you, Val? Hmm?"

Alana pressed her hand against the side of Val's face. It took everything in Val not to moan and press her face into Alana's palm.

Val brushed her hand away.

"Never have."

"Never will. Last time I heard anything about the Splinter of Heaven, Idris, that diamond cutter out of Johannesburg was commissioned to turn it into 3 stones. Hence the name, Tears of the Son. Like the Trinity: Father, Son, Holy Spirit."

"Both of your kids are fine, Alana." Val said as she took her hand.

Alana ran a thumb over her bare ring finger.

"If you want my head clear, that topic is not up for discussion."

"So, you don't want to know if..."

Alana turned back to her.

"You didn't need to bring them into this." She tossed the blanket back and looked at her ankle. "If you wanted something from me, all you had to do was ask."

Val blinked rapidly as she fixed the blanket.

"That was all Phae. I'd never use the kids against you. Anyway, I got Monet home, and the cop found your son. Phaedra thought..."

"I'm sure she did."

"Hey!" Val yelled, "Don't do that. Don't talk bad about her."

"Or what, Val?"

Val stood up and fixed the sheet back over Alana's cast.

"I gave you my word. Phae didn't. She has her own people that don't mind walking up to a door and shooting someone through the peephole."

"Then I guess we need to stay on task, huh? She ever tell you what I did to make her hate me so much?"

Val hazarded a glance before continuing to tuck the sheets around Alana.

"No. Just keeps saying you know what you did."

"Then you know about as much as I do. When does the cast come off?"

"You'll still need a week or two of physical therapy, and there's something else." Val's gaze dropped to the duvet. She moved to pull the blanket up to her shoulder. Alana blocked her hand.

"Like Phae gives a shit. She wants the stones, right? Well I need to get back on my feet before Phae decides to dispatch someone to put a bullet through my front door."

Val walked over to the door blinking back tears.

"I never wanted this, Alana, not any of it. If you had come to me that night like we planned."

"I came to you when William died."

Val turned and looked at her.

"Whispers…William begged for you in the end. He wasn't right until he saw you. Then, he died, and you left us *again*." Val leaned in the doorway as a wave of nausea hit her. "I knew you'd fight to keep your son safe, but I never wanted you to get back into this."

"Doesn't matter what either of us wants, apparently."

Val opened the door then closed it again as the room greyed away. She gave her head a sharp shake.

"You were all I…." Val bit down on the last part and started again. "Cast comes off in two days. Write down the museums in the order you think best."

CHAPTER 26

By the time Cass left Harvey Knox's villa, he was numb. Going back to the Consulate was out of the question. Levine would pepper him with questions that Cass wasn't sure he wanted to answer just yet.

In the span of an evening he had found out more about Alana than she had told him in all the years he'd been married to her. The shifting sands that had been his wife for all those years settled in his mind, creating a portrait of a stranger.

He sat in his hotel room watching the footage of Knox and Isla sitting across from Alana in the visitor's room. The first visit had just been the three of them staring at each other through the thermoplastic. Knox's hair was just starting to grey, and Isla, swaddled in a white shawl, looked as regal as Alana did. Cass could make out a long black braid that snaked between the older woman's shoulders.

From where he sat on his bed, he could see the Eiffel Tower bathed in white light that seemed to caress the sky. In the months since Alana's disappearance and the sudden return of Monet, the leads were going cold. Just then the telephone in his suite rang. Cass walked over and picked it up.

"Speak."

"Cass, it's Mark."

Cass sat down on the bed.

"You guys okay back there? Kids okay?"

"Everybody is fine. I'm calling to check on you. Tell me everything."

"What's to tell? I have the rings I put on my wife's hand in my pocket and a big gaping hole at my side where she should be standing."

"The Feds don't have any leads?"

"They've all dried up, and I don't think they care anymore."

"Cass, I'm sure that's not..."

"What, true? Alana scares them even now. They mentioned her name at the Consulate. I wish you could have heard the hush in that building. We were ordered into a meeting with both the former and current President. I got the feeling that they didn't want her found."

"What about Harvey Knox and Isla Ado?"

Cass winced at the sounds of their names. It was still too close. Not once had Alana spoken of meeting with them or that they were her parents. Christ, did she even know or was that withheld from her like every other human kindness.

Not once had she spoken about taking their son to meet these people. Cass wasn't angry so much as he felt left out, as if there was an entire world that Alana lived and breathed in that simply did not include him.

"Yeah, I spoke with Knox. Hey, is that puzzle box still on the kitchen table where I left it?"

"Yeah, why?"

"Take a look at the box for me."

Mark's voice faded as he went to retrieve the box.

"You looking at it?

"Yeah, looks like one of those old teach me puzzles from the 60s. Didn't know you guys liked jigsaw puzzles. No pieces in the box though."

Cass caressed the papers and passports in the breast pocket of his jacket.

"Describe the box."

"It's in pretty good condition for its age. It's got museums from all over the world on the cover. No pieces, like I said. Gabe's got toys in it. Typical kid stuff. Why, does it mean anything?"

Cass swallowed hard as he tried to fit the pieces together. It was too much to hope for, and he couldn't afford to say much because he was sure his phone was wired.

She'd put something in something that looked insignificant. She'd hide it in plain sight.

The words washed through him, making him feel nauseous.

"Cass, you alright, man?"

"Gabe kept getting holes in his pants pockets because he filled them with toy cars and army men. Alana probably gave him the box for his toys." Cass cleared his throat and tucked the phone between his shoulder and his ear. The air in the room seemed thinner as he remembered going through the box back home.

When they returned home with Monet, Cass went back to the box and emptied it. He'd been carrying the papers and passports on him since.

He even watched as Gabe started bringing little cars and action figures to the table to play, and just before Cass announced that it was bedtime Gabe gathered his toys, put them in the box and closed the lid. Cass pushed the box over to him, and Gabe shook his head and pushed it back.

"I'll wait till Mom gets back. She may need my box again."

"Alright man, is there anything you need?"

Mark's voice cut through the memory as Cass gripped the phone in his fist. "Nah. Make sure Gabe brushes his teeth. Is Monet eating?"

"Just barely. Myra is bout ready to start spoon feeding her. Gabe is no better, clings to her like a spider monkey. They're just quiet. I asked if there was anything you needed?

Cass took in a deep breath then let it rush through his teeth.

"I need that day in my kitchen back, when all my wife wanted was…." He bit down on the last part, regretting so much. Cass took in a breath that hurt entirely too much. "Hell, I need my whole goddammed life with her back. I mean, she's been telling me all along, and I didn't listen."

"Cass." Mark started and then sighed.

"I need Alana." Cass ran his hand over his close-cropped hair.

The words sounded simple enough, and God knew it was the truth, but there was more to it. Alana was so woven into the fabric of his being, he scarcely knew where he started and she began. He thought about his chair in the kitchen and the mornings he spent making love to her with the smell of coffee and burnt toast or bacon in the air.

"Well, I don't know if this helps, but I've been in Cold Cases and Juvie all day drilling down on the years Julian Barlow was into pros."

"Find anything?"

"Not sure, but there was an incident way back. Alana had to be twelve or thirteen. There was this strip of highway connecting three states."

"I remember, Mark, cops back then called it Silk Road. It was the way they transported girls back and forth."

"Well, apparently another road ran parallel, only it was made to get them out. Well all hell broke loose one night at one of the safehouses. Some kid called in a tip. People packed in a house like sardines. Cops get there and virtually every inch of linoleum in that place had a person sitting on it. Kids as young as five mixed in with the women. And in the very middle of them was this nasty bit of work named Phaedra Khalid."

"Phaedra Khalid…." Cass stared out the window at the traffic rushing by. "Alana ran her and some other girls. She even helped a few get out of The Life. Phaedra Khalid may have been one of them."

"Well, that kid rode the back of this town like a witch. Made her shit obvious. Calls herself a businesswoman now. Social media eats her up like she's a cool hunter."

"A what? Listen to yourself, Mark."

"Kids on my squad keep me young. Cool hunters know who's drinking or drugging and wearing what. Who got dicked down or cock blocked and who's who in the legit industry and the underground. She's got followers that think she's God squared. Bitch might even believe it herself. I'll keep drilling down and get wit you later. You need to wrap this up, Cass. Your kids look like zombies."

"I'm trying, Mark."

CHAPTER 27

After Mark hung up Cass pulled the laptop over to his side and keyed in a password to take him back to Google and the list of museums in Europe. His phone buzzed again, and he pushed the call button. At once, Levine's voice filled the line.

"Where the hell have you been? Did you talk to Knox? What did he say? Is Alana alive? You know that was a stupid move. The man could have killed you."

Cass scrolled through the names of the people in the picture as he listened to Levine's tirade. "Knox has no desire to kill me. He claims he was helping us search for Alana."

"And you believe him? The man is a habitual liar and a traitor."

"Aren't we all?" Cass mused.

"What? Look, open the door; I'm outside."

Cass listened for the line to go dead as he closed his laptop. He opened the door, and Levine walked in.

"Nicholas, what do you know about a woman named Phaedra Khalid?"

"Khalid is a businesswoman from the states that moved her enterprises overseas. She's into high fashion, drugs, whores, usual freak shit. Khalid has an import and export business that looks legit from the outside, but Interpol and a few other agencies have her on their watch lists."

Cass went back to his laptop, cleared the museums from his screen, and typed in Phaedra's name. He started to scroll through the files that were available on the woman.

"Apparently, she was publicly tossed out on her ass after a botched robbery attempt at some rich duke's place in some country nobody ever heard of. The next time anybody heard of her, she was shaking her moneymaker in a brothel in Lisbon. You still haven't said how this ties into Alana."

"I don't know that it does, I'm just asking questions," Cass said. He watched as his old agency partner sighed and looked down at the table.

"Cass..." Levine moved his long-forgotten Styrofoam coffee cup around in a circle before he finally looked up at him.

Cass let his gaze drift to Levine's face. "I already know."

"It's just we have things brewing back in the States and I think we've overstayed our welcome here. I already spoke to brass, if she is alive and she pulls anything, her gratis is gone. There are no golden parachutes this time. They are talking hard time, especially if she's in league with the likes of Khalid and her organization."

Cass sat back in the chair and grabbed his own mug. "After all she's done. After all she gave you people. I thought the bug Isla and Knox put in people's ears had progeny."

"Five minutes ago is 10 years too late. The reach Isla and Knox had...those men are either pissing in bags or on oxygen. The world has changed, Cass."

"Devil will have his due."

"Cass, try to understand."

"Go home, Levine, it's fine, but I have to stay."

"You can't do this alone. Like I said, we have a presence."

"When I met Alana I was pretty much alone."

"This is different."

"How is it different, Nicholas? Alana is the only woman I know that will walk into an impossible situation with no expectation that someone is going to ride in on a white horse to save her. Whether it was beaten or bred into her, Alana knows how to travel light in this world. She owns things, loves things, but they don't own her. Alana could walk away if she had to."

"From you? From the kids?"

"If she thought it would keep us safe…." Cass swallowed hard at the clump of emotion crowding his throat. "To keep us alive… yeah."

"That's a flimsy reason to stay, Cass, even for you. Did you ever stop to think that she may have left because she wanted to? If she's with this Phaedra Khalid, how do you know she didn't want to come home? These are her people...her kind."

Cass managed a smile. "Alana never wanted to inflict her demons on me, begged me to walk away so many times, but I exacted a promise from her. Made the same promise to her. Nobody leaves."

"With her wedding bands in your pocket, you really think she's kept her word?"

"Our entire marriage is built on trust. It took years for Alana to trust me. I owe her that grace."

"She didn't trust you with all of this," Levine said quietly. "I'm just saying."

Cass reached in his pocket and pulled out the rings. "I don't deserve these."

Levine leaned closer. "What?"

"It's what Alana said when I placed these on her hand. There was no engagement, I just... She played jacks with gemstones worth millions of dollars, and my rings mattered more to her than anything in the world. After everything she went through, everything I put her through to solve a case. To make a career, as you said. Maybe it's me that doesn't deserve..."

"Cass…" Levine started.

Cass blinked away the memory, and he closed his hand over the rings. "Alana doesn't break promises. She doesn't know how."

* * *

Harvey Knox glanced in his rearview mirror as he made his way along the narrow road that led back to his villa. The place where he'd met Cass was his place too, but there were too many memories there, too many ghosts. With enough wine or vodka in his system, Harvey could almost convince himself that Isla was sitting in her chair in the library reading one of her books. But then the holes would appear in his fantasy, and the dream would reduce to Knox cradling Isla in his arms as she tried to breathe past the air that was flooding her chest and crushing her ribs. Isla had been late returning from her errands. It didn't take him long to discover her overturned vehicle.

"Alana was my masterpiece. Splinter was hers. The Tears were hers."

Cancer took her away from me. Even then the lie slid easily from his throat. It was true that the doctors had given Isla only a few more months, but that wasn't what killed her. As she called for Alana with the last breaths she took, Knox knew that his end was getting closer.

Harvey made his way up to the cabin and coasted to a stop. He tested the air around him and smiled. The stench of gun oil and marijuana tinged the air. He climbed out of the car and made his way up to the house. Knox didn't struggle when he felt them descend on him. He didn't call out when he felt the thump and the brilliant flash of pain between his shoulder blades.

"Isla..." he mumbled as the world went black.

CHAPTER 28

Getting into the bank and down into the vaults was child's play. As much as technology had changed the face of security, there were always traditionalists that felt that the old ways were infinitely better. In some cases, Alana agreed. As she made her way through the tunnels and catacombs under the city of Paris, the world moved on. People moved on as money and other riches changed hands above her, but the sewer system and the mosaic of skulls fused to the floor and the walls were still very much the same. Down there, death smelled sweet.

As a novice, she had cringed at the sight of rats scurrying about and nearly passed out from the fear when her first crew lost her in one of the tunnels. She spent three days below the city starving while she searched for the way out. As an old pro, the rats were almost companions. Alana merely followed them away from the constant trickle of fetid water to a place where the air smelled fresher.

"Can't sit down... can't fall asleep. They start biting when you do," she said to no one in particular.

"Still remember, Isla. I was down here so long it became home. After a while I don't know if it was madness or starvation that made me want to be here. Phaedra couldn't stay... wouldn't stay. I remember when we trained. It was too much for her. She cried so hard because she didn't like being dirty. Down here no one ever wanted to follow. It was why I chose that building in the slaughter district in Shadow Bay.

The blood and the screams had leached into the walls. Couldn't remember if they belonged to the animals or me, but it was home. It was quiet there. Cass found me there more than once after everything was over. He didn't understand, and I couldn't tell him.

Even the woods where I left my son... it was quiet there, full of secrets lies and silence that lasting quiet that grew" she murmured as she climbed hand over hand out of the sewer and into a hallway that led into one of the subterranean shops beneath the Louvre. From a short distance she could hear the tinkling of glass as the sound of music and tourists moving through the shops reminded her of her assignment.

Alana stepped into the bathroom stall where she'd left a change of clothing stashed behind a commode. She quickly scrubbed the grime from her skin and slipped into the housekeeping uniform she'd pilfered from a locker days before. She followed some of the other people from the cleaning crew past the checkpoints. She stopped briefly to polish one of the display cases as she looked up at the artwork. She breathed in the quiet and tilted her head as the painting of the Mona Lisa stared down on her with her knowing eyes.

"Hello, old friend," Alana whispered.

* * *

Val eased herself into the chair just inside Knox's cabin. She watched as her men dragged the man inside.

"Search the place. See if it's here."

"Val, what if it's not here?" Brian asked quietly in the dark.

"He knows where it is; make him talk!"

"And if he doesn't?" Brian asked as he stooped to rest his hand on her knee. "Val, what if he doesn't know? Isla was..."

"Isla was an accident." Val jerked away from him so fast that she hit her head against the wall. He reached for her once more. "Pity is a wasted emotion, little brother. I just need this all to end."

She took out her handkerchief and swabbed at her nose. She looked at the cloth with disgust as she settled back in the chair.

"If Knox doesn't know and Alana can't find it, then what was all of this for?"

Val glared down on him as she wiped her nose again. "Don't say her name."

"Why bring Alana into this at all, if all we had to do was come find Knox and make him talk."

"Don't say her name!"

Brian glanced over his shoulder at his men tying Knox to a chair. The men had stopped what they were doing when Val raised her voice.

"You know I saw you stow that jump out bag on the balcony for Alana. If you're going to help her escape then why even..." Brian gestured with his head for them to continue, as he turned to face Val.

She sat up so that she was face to face with him. Her eyes glittered with a murderous hate as she looked down at him. The blood that dripped from her nostrils in fine runnels made her look even more savage.

"Stay in your lane, little brother. Alana will do what she was built to do, and Phaedra will manipulate just enough to make people think it was their idea."

"Is that what she did with you, Val? That why you married her? You hated her in the beginning. What did she say to you on the tarmac all those years ago? You were sick with pneumonia, half dead with cold; waiting for Alana to show up."

Val pressed her forehead to Brian's and sighed. "Please don't make me kill you to shut you up."

Brian jerked away from her, but Val hooked a hand around his neck and brought him closer. The smell of death on Val was so strong that Brian cleared his throat and struggled not to gag.

"Alana will do what she was trained to do. Now make him talk. It's why we were sent here in the event she can't find what she's looking for in the vaults at the Louvre. Now get the fuck out of my sight."

Val settled back in the dark and scrubbed at her nose once more.

CHAPTER 29

Alana sat down in the shower and let the near scalding water beat down on her as it filled the bathroom with steam. She scrubbed herself raw, waiting for the warmth to return to her center. The longer she sat under the spray, the more she thought of home and the last time she'd been in a shower.

At the beginning of their marriage clothing didn't seem like an option. Early mornings found them sitting in the middle of their bed with her seated on his muscular thighs and her legs folded around him. Often she had his face in her hands as she traced his lips with her thumb or her tongue.

Back then everything was intimate, from the way they shared a bowl of berries for breakfast in bed to the various places they made love all throughout his apartment. Those first hot, sticky nights on his balcony in one of his chairs, or against the glass door in the kitchen, made her skin blush and the pearl at the top of her thighs throb.

Over the years Cass became a very tactile man, as if his perception of reality was based more on her proximity to him than the rest of his senses. When he walked into the house he didn't call for her, he simply found her and held her. When they were in bed he seemed to sleep better when one or both of his arms were around her. Rarely did she use her pillow. Even in his sleep, he would pull her closer or lift her from the place at his side and drape her over his body like a blanket. His heartbeat was her primitive lullaby.

Even as they stood in the kitchen before, she went to pick up their son from school, Cass held her, hugging her more with his body than his arms. And then there was the gentle, worshipping way he made love to her. Never the same, always searching her eyes for any discomfort or fear.

Can I have you?

Never once in all their years together had he assumed that his touch was welcome or wanted. Even after she asked him to stop asking, the words carried more on breath than sound sealed the breaks in her heart like veins of gold.

Alana ran her hand between her thighs and winced at the absence of him. She moved her hand to her breast and then her mouth, remembering the rasp of his beard and the intensity of his touch.

There wasn't a place on her body his mouth hadn't been, and the lack of him made her throat close with unshed tears. She looked down at her bare left hand resting on her midsection. The tan line from her wedding rings made her burst into tears as she turned her face into the hot spray from the showerhead.

* * *

Alana slowly shrugged into the white terrycloth robe on the back of the bathroom door while opening the patio door to allow the frigid Parisian evening air in before settling on the queen-sized bed. She looked around the room once more, taking in the decidedly male décor. Alana walked over to the massive library that spanned entire walls. Each shelf held leather-bound classics with gold lettering on the spines.

You were all I ever…

Val's words still hung in the air like an accusation. After all these years, Val's feelings hadn't changed. Everything in the room spoke of that quiet painful truth.

As her cut person, Val stitched wounds and set broken bones for Alana. She prayed that with each injury Val would come to see her as a piece of equipment that needed routine maintenance, but her touch never changed. It lingered over Alana's wounds as if to work compassion and an apology into her broken skin. But then it would come out in conversation.

"I know your body better than anybody."

The pride she heard in Val's voice, the possessive tone, made her think about the Mona Lisa hanging in the gallery. There was more behind the words, more behind the smile. Even as she sat by Phaedra's side when Alana first came down to dinner, it was there.

Val's eyes glittered as her gaze slipped in and out of the plumes of smoke. She had the best of both worlds around her. Alana shoved her hand through her hair and made a fist. The longer she sat at the dinner table with Phaedra glaring at her over the candle sticks, the more Alana knew how much the woman was seething inside.

Even as the server came to the table with the skull shaped goblet and bowl of sugar cubes and absinthe for Val and the two ice-choked Styrofoam cups and bottle of vodka for Phaedra, it hung in the air.

The jealousy, the envy, all-consuming desire to bring Alana down to her level so that she could ask…. *Where did it go left? What makes you so special?*

Even there, Val seemed to postpone the age-old war.

"Alana doesn't drink. Get that out of here. Bring her some orange juice or iced tea. You still drink green tea, right?"

Alana shook away the memories as she picked up the dossier she'd pulled from the vault. She turned it over in her hands once more before she willed herself to open it and look at the contents.

Inside were photos of Isla and Knox and newspaper clippings from Isla's heists. Alana's eyes welled with tears as she ran her hand over the pictures. The last time she'd seen Isla was just before she'd been released from prison. Isla had sat on the floor with Alana and smoothed her hands over Alana's face and hair.

"I don't understand how you got in here," Alana said.

"I taught you how to get into impossible places, didn't I?" Isla smiled as she marveled over Alana's face.

"Isla…"

"The Splinter of Heaven was yours even after they cut it into pieces. Apart the pieces will take care of you and the cop and your children and theirs. Together they are more than the Hope Diamond."

"But what if I don't want it?"

Isla hissed as she pulled her hands from Alana's face. "It is your birthright! It was foolish to put those girls in your place, The Rose Gold network you created to get them out of The Life only thrived because I thought you were coming home to me. Instead, you kept sending other children, other people. Why did you stay in Shadow Bay, child?"

"There were others I couldn't just leave behind, Isla. Some were younger than me, others older but weaker. Someone had to stay behind."

"Why did it have to be you? I posted bail. I made sure there was enough."

"All except one. She got busted for boosting a car. Foster care found a family for her brother because he was younger. She was always left behind. So, I made a choice."

"Ralph Austin, the old police Lt in Shadow Bay, did things to you. He allowed others to…"

"He died in prison, Isla. It's over."

"Yes, and he died screaming. They couldn't get the smell of his burning flesh out of that pod for weeks. You thought Dominic did all the other killings. I did my fair share." The sneer contorting Isla's face made Alana reach for her.

Isla rose to her feet and gripped Alana's arm to steady herself but fell and Alana caught her.

"Let me call for help…."

Isla placed her forehead against Alana's.

"Buffer's gone now. Not that I was ever an effective one for you. The Splinter of Heaven has been reduced to Tears. Three distinct stones. They are yours, Alana, they always were.

Alana shook away the memory as she gathered the paperwork back into the folder. By then Phaedra was standing in the doorway watching her. The stench of her gardenia perfume filled the air.

CHAPTER 30

"The Splinter How did you find out about the Splinter, Phaedra?"

Phaedra came in and leaned against the dresser. She caught a glimpse of herself in the mirror and straightened her clothes and smoothed down her blonde braids.

"Julian said he read about it in one of your history books."

"Wasn't in any history book, Phae. Julian was obsessed with the idea of it. Marvin Caine told him about it."

"Well, that's where you and your trip to the bank this evening comes in. You covered yourself well, blowing those other boxes and taking the contents. Gave me enough dirt on some key people to keep me in paper for many years to come. It's what I loved most about your work, Alana. You were always so thorough. Never a half-ass job with you."

"Wasn't enough though, was it? It's never enough for you." Alana closed the folder and clutched it to her chest.

Phaedra came away from the dresser so quickly that she almost looked like she was going to fall. "It was mine! And just like everything else, you stole it from me!"

"What are you talking about? I haven't taken anything—"

"Julian loved me first! I was in his stable *first*. I could steal, too!"

"You couldn't stand the sewers, Phaedra, remember? You almost had a nervous breakdown when Julian ordered us down there for training. The roaches, the rats, and the sewage made you scream,"

"Julian forgave me for that! He understood. I tried to bring you and those other girls to him, but you and that dumb priest stood in the way. Julian liked the fact that you resisted him for so long. He told me so. He liked it so much that he started devoting every waking moment to acquiring you, and I got swept to the side. He gave you my room. He threw me out because of you!"

"You mean to tell me this is all about…?"

"I was pregnant with Julian's child *first*! He made me get rid of it, but he let you keep yours. He married you, gave you a name... *my* name!"

"Marriage? You have no concept. It was more like slavery. I wasn't a wife; I was a tool. You lament something that never was. And what about your other children? I know that Val adopted some."

"Foot soldiers. After the abortion I couldn't have anymore, feed a few orphans, clothe a few pros, and you got yourself an army. Treat em like shit long enough then give them something sweet. They'll think you're God. Isn't that what Harvey Knox taught us? Have you figured out where your next heist is, Alana? Harvey Knox is also a talker for the right price."

Alana set the file aside and rose from the bed. "Leave him out of this. You wanted me here; you have me here. My family is off limits. He is an old man, and he's done—"

"Nothing, but get hurt really bad for not telling me where the stones are."

Alana lunged at Phaedra, and they both fell to the floor. Phaedra wrestled Alana onto her back and dug her knee into Alana's midsection.

"You still don't get it do you, Alana? I run this. I can get you where you live, unless you do exactly what I say, when I say. And you thought Julian knew how to make you cry. I can make you scream."

Alana managed to pull her legs up to her chest and plant her feet in Phaedra's midsection. She summoned all the strength she had and extended her legs. Phaedra fell back just far enough for Alana to roll over and push herself to her feet. She took off running across the room toward the window.

"Kill her!" Phaedra screamed.

As she neared the window, Alana saw others enter the room and it erupted into gunfire. Alana dove through the open glass door and landed on the patio. She got up and launched herself at the ivy-covered latticework that lined each side of the doorway. Alana mentally followed the map to the top of the building that she had laid out days before. Val, seeming to predict Alana's next move, had hidden a jump out bag for her. And as she made her way down the side of the mansion and off into the woods, she could hear Phaedra inside screaming.

* * *

By the time she reached Knox's villa the first rays of sunlight were pouring through the clouds. Alana made her way through the back entrance to find the place ransacked. She was almost through the darkened living quarters when she heard Knox coughing in the corner. She found a lamp and turned it on. The chair he had been tied to was overturned, and the old man was on his back. His blue eyes stared back at her.

"There's my girl."

Alana tried to wipe away the blood on his face as she suppressed a sob.

"Shh. It's okay. I told them I didn't have it. Didn't believe me."

"Knox, don't talk. I'm gonna get you out of here." She managed to get his hands untied as she pulled him into her lap.

"Don't give away your birthright, Alana."

"Please, Knox. I don't even know where it is. They can have it for all I care."

"Your Mamma gave it to me to hold, but I was weak. I sold it off. It's changed hands twice that I know of."

"I don't care, Knox."

"You have to care because she won't leave it to rest. Phaedra will keep coming after you until she has it."

"But I don't have it! I never did."

"Shhh... Shhh. Don't, Alana. Your mother knew I'd sell it. I don't know how she managed it, but she took it back."

"From whom... to where?"

"Where it all began, Alana. Your siblings are buried in the burning sand, but the stones... there are three now. Father... Son... Holy Spirit," Knox said as he rummaged with his left hand under a pile of papers and an overturned table. Alana watched as he withdrew a handkerchief and a gun and placed it on his chest.

"I can't be here without her, Alana. I tried."

"No, Knox, I can get you help." She tried to smooth down his shirt, and he pushed the handkerchief into her hand. He tried to do the same with the gun, but Alana kept pushing it away.

"I trained you. You know how these things end. You know what I'm asking!"

"No. I can get you help. They can fix you; they can."

"So, they can come back and keep asking? Anymore and I would have told them anything...Museum Island, The Book of Kells, hell, even the Walters Art Gallery in Maryland. The stones could be in any one of them. I thought it would bring me to my Isla, so I sold you out. Leave, Cuishle. Leave, sweetheart. I can't be here anymore. Not without her. Not without my Isla. Go on…"

CHAPTER 31

"Val, she's here." Brian put a hand on Val's shoulder "We should probably get out of here."

"Why. She'll know it was us either way." Val sat up in the passenger seat of the van parked across the street. "Loved boosting cars with her. We'd just drive. She always gave me the other half of her sandwich or the other cupcake in the pack."

"She killed our father, Valerie."

"No, she didn't. Dad killed himself because everyone knew what he was doing to the kids at the church."

"And to us, but no one stopped it until Alana got us out of there." "Was where she took us any better than you on the streets and me in foster care?"

"They weren't going to take us both, Brian. Alana kept me clean and safe."

"She turned you out."

Val sat up in her seat.

"Phaedra did that, made me think of it as business because I was good at giving head. Her motto was, 'Sell your talents.'"

Val removed her headphones and watched as Alana stepped out into the morning light. A single gunshot rocked the air, and Alana screamed and fell to her knees.

* * *

Cass stood by the sidelines with the rest of the spectators watching the police go in and out of the bank. Levine finally reappeared, and he jogged over to Cass.

"Well?"

Levine lifted the crime tape, and they headed back into the building. They walked over to the elevators that led to the vaults and the safe-deposit boxes.

"Never seen anything like it. Nothing on the top level was disturbed, camera alarm systems are fine; everything is intact. Forensics is in there, and they think they came up out of the sewer system somehow. What I can't figure out, is how they walked past the cameras down there. For a minute they could track a heat signature, but even that made no sense. It just looked like rats scurrying across the floor."

Cass took in a shaky breath; it was too much to hope for.

"Alana... when she worked with us... with Teacher. She told me about a suit. Something that could refract light, distort heat signatures. I was only in on one of the heists where Alana used that suit. I watched her move. Scared the hell out of me."

"From what I read about that, she wouldn't allow anyone but you in the vault with her, or even on that floor. Why?"

"She wanted me to see her. Not the mystique or the myth or the legend the agency wove around her, just her."

Just then an Interpol agent walked up. "You are the husband, no? Well what do you think? Is it her?'

Cass walked over to the safety deposit box area and looked inside. He was about to straighten up when it hit him, so strongly that he fell shoulder first into the wall and slid down. Levine rushed over to him.

"Cass, what is it?"

Cass rolled over and pressed his back against the wall. He waved off the paramedics and pulled Levine closer. "Alana is hurt…I don't know…she's in pain, terrible pain."

The Interpol agent walked into the vault then came back. "Is it your wife? She is the one, no?" Cass gripped Levine's shoulder, and the man helped him to his feet. Levine shook his arm. "Cass was it her," he whispered?

Cass shook his head wildly as he assumed his full height and turned to the Interpol agent. "Call off your dogs. My wife isn't here."

* * *

At the airport, Levine stood by Cass as they both looked out the window to watch the aircrafts taxiing to and from the runway. The skycaps were busy refueling, storing luggage, or pushing the portable staircases up to the private jets.

"Since we left the scene, there's been talk of a break-in at the prison where Alana did her time."

"They find anything, Nicholas?"

"Not a thing. I think you should come back to the States. "

He turned to Levine and smiled. "You know I can't do that. My children need their mother."

"And what about you, Cass?"

Cass took in a deep breath and smiled. "I need a time when my wife's unfinished business is all about me. I know how it sounds after everything I put her through."

Levine looked beyond Cass to see one of his men waving him over. "Our presence here is still strong. I reached out to some friends of mine. They aren't agency anymore, but they know the landscape. Brian Mitchell is a friend. He can help you get places most people can't."

"I'll call him if I need to."

"Actually, he called me. Brian has an in. He's Phaedra's wife's brother.

There's a party coming up in Italy. Apparently, Phaedra is throwing a birthday bash for her wife."

"You trust him?"

"Man is one of the best turncoats we've got." Levine shook Cass's hand and walked away.

CHAPTER 32

Alana stared at the balcony doors. Someone had come in while she was gone and boarded them up. The glass and splintered wood had been swept up, but she didn't venture near the door. She crouched on the bed near the journals that Val had placed on her lap when Brian finally managed to gather her up and put her in the back of the van. The second she saw the van, Alana rose to her feet and started walking toward it. She got around to Val's door, yanked it open and slapped her in the face. Alana then felt someone come up behind her and hit her in the head from behind. The last thing Alana heard was Val screaming, '*no*'.

Alana winced at the hard lump on the back of her head. A nurse had been in and out all-day bringing food and pain medicine, all of which Alana refused. Val only came to the door once. She leaned on the doorsill while two nurses held Alana down and administered the pain medication and started an IV. Once they finished, Val ordered them out of the room.

Val went over to the bed and busied herself with checking Alana's pulse and running a hand over her midsection. Then she sat on the bed and gingerly touched the lump on the back of Alana's head.

"I know you hate me," Val started. "For a long time, I tried to hate you because I waited for you, and you didn't come home."

"Val..." Alana started.

Val rested her fingers over Alana's mouth then she scrubbed her own mouth with the same hand.

"My plans never changed, Alana. I waited for you."

"And Phaedra?"

"Phaedra understood me... wanted me."

Alana tugged at the cloth ties that held her to the bed. Val untied her wrist. Alana raised her hand to Val's face and watched as she winced but didn't pull away.

"I'm sorry I hit you," Alana said softly.

"I deserved it. I keep taking people from you, hurting you." Val murmured as she turned her mouth into Alana's palm.

"Check the pocket of my clothes." Alana said softly.

Val looked around the room until she found Alana's clothes in a heap in the corner. She rifled through the pockets and came back with a handkerchief. Val sank down on the bed as she unfolded the cloth. She bit back a yelp as the brilliantly clear stone caught the light in the room, making it shimmer.

"Knox was very good at talking a good game when he thought he was being listened to."

Alana's hand came to rest on Val's cheek once more. Val looked at her.

"How did we come to this, Val? You were supposed to be this brilliant doctor, and I was going to be a social worker. Both of us trying to save the world in our own way."

Val leaned down and pressed her forehead against Alana's. She breathed her in deep before she pressed her lips to the shimmering tear that had spilled back into Alana's hairline.

"Plans change, Alana." Val whispered. "I didn't want to hurt him. I never wanted to kill him; you have to know that."

"Stop. You can't take it back any more than I can. He wanted to die." Alana turned over on her side so that her back was to Val. She huddled into a ball. "And so, did my mother Isla."

"Alana..." she started, but Alana folded herself into a tighter ball. "Alana please look at me. I need to say this.... I need you to hear me... see me say this, because Isla didn't have to die the way she did."

Alana was quiet for a long time. She sighed and turned over onto her back. Val straightened the blankets around her. Alana stilled her hands.

"You can't take that one back either, Val. I want to go home. I need to get back to my family."

"I know," Val started. "There are times when I can't control her."

"Nobody could control Phaedra, not even Julian. Take the stone to her. Maybe it's enough to set us both free."

"I'm not a prisoner, Alana." Val shook her head as she smoothed out the blanket over the soft swell of Alana's abdomen. Her dark brown eyes shimmered. A tear stole down her cheek.

Alana brushed it away. "Sure, about that?"

"She won't rest, and I have to stay here. Alana, there's more...."

Alana winced as she pushed herself into a seated position. She clutched at her lower abdomen where Phaedra had dug in her knee.

"Guggenheim Venice should be next. Judging by the way Isla had photographed that old puzzle box, I think we need to look there. I've already been through the scenario with the group. I can't stress enough they've gotta follow my lead. If I tell them to abort, I don't need dissensions in the ranks. They'll get killed if they get greedy."

"Done."

"No one should follow me to the vault. I cut the power and blow the boxes, but no one goes in with me. If it's there, I'll bring it, and any other papers I find, out of there."

Val sat quietly, fixing the blankets around Alana once more.

"I can feel them pulling at me. I can feel Cass moving through me. Valerie, please let me go home."

As she drifted off, Alana felt Val fix the blankets once more before she walked out.

CHAPTER 33

Phaedra peered into the mirror as she smeared on more lip gloss. She directed her gaze to the bed where Val had been resting for hours. More than once, Phaedra had walked over to the bed to check on her and fix the blankets around her. The last time Phaedra walked over and busied herself on Val's bedside table trying to rearrange the medication bottles, Val cracked one of her eyes enough to study Phaedra.

"Get the fuck away from me."

"I know you're tired, and this last bit of business took a lot out of you."

"What did I just say? Do I have to leave this room to get you to leave me alone?"

"And where would you go, Val? Let me guess, to sit in your old room with her?"

"Can't do that, now can I? You shot it full of holes. There are bullet holes in my fucking books, Phaedra, and then there was a shitload of glass on the floor. What if she'd been hurt or worse? She was clutching her midsection in her sleep. What did you do?"

"She started it." She said meekly. "I only wanted to."

"I did an ultrasound. If you had hurt either one of them."

"You act like the twins she's carrying are yours."

"Phae, I'm tired."

Phaedra smoothed her hand over Val's cheek.

"I can still kill her you know."

"True that, but then you wouldn't have the rest of your precious stones, now would you?" Val cracked an eye and stared at her.

"Still don't have them. You left our bed to sit in there and watch her sleep. Saw you once. Resting your head on the pillow above hers. Only thing you didn't do is climb in with her."

"Alana had double pneumonia, Phaedra. She's already stopped breathing in the night once."

"And one of the many nurses and doctors I have on standby for you couldn't go in there with her? I can still do it to her, you know. Will do it if you don't stop going in there with her."

"And if you do, I follow her."

"You don't even know what she said to me, yet you always take her side."

Val reached over and dragged Phaedra closer to the bed. "I just ordered my people to beat an old man within an inch of his life for you. Then, I got to listen to that same old man blow his own head off because he wanted to be with Alana's mother. The same woman I had Brian run off the goddamned road! So let's not discuss what side I'm on."

Val let Phaedra's wrist go and settled back down in the bed. Val turned over onto her side and looked over at their bedroom door as she ran her hand under her nose, and it came back bloody. She muttered a curse.

"You shouldn't have let her hit you. At the very least I could have..."

Val turned over to see Phaedra flip her blonde hair back from her face as she smoothed her pinky over her bottom lip.

"The way you keep a close watch on her... the way you touch her. You never did that when I was pregnant."

"As if you really gave a shit, Phaedra. I wanted a baby. We had the in vitro. The docs found a way. You drank and drugged so much that I was glad when you miscarried, but all of that has jack shit to do with why you pulled a gun on Alana this evening. So, let's not muddy the water. You have one of the stones now. Just that one makes you richer than God. Knox must have had it stashed somewhere and waited for Alana, and she gave it to us."

"Correction, she gave the stone to *you*."

"Fuck difference does it make, Phaedra?! You have one!"

Val pulled the blanket over her head and turned her face into the pillow.

"Happy Birthday, by the way."

Val pulled the blanket from her face. Phaedra turned so that Val got a good view of her ass cheeks peeking from under her towel.

"I had your outfit ironed. There's even a crisp white baseball cap waiting for you. This new club is legit, and after tonight it will be on the map."

Val stared at the ceiling. She thought back to the ride back to the compound with Alana thrown in a heap in the back of the van. She left the passenger seat and sat in the back holding an icepack to the back of Alana's head.

"I owe you one for hitting her Brian."

"She shouldn't have hit you."

Val leaned over and spat in a wad of facial tissue.

"I'm not going to any club tonight, Phae, as you can see, I'm occupied."

"But it's your birthday. I planned for this party weeks ago."

"Phae, look at me. The bleeding is worse. The cancer is in my blood now. I'm losing teeth. The blood transfusions barely keep my iron levels normal."

Phaedra tried to tuck the blanket around Val, but she caught her hand and snuggled down against it. She watched a tear drop from her butterfly wing framed eye. Val reached up and traced the wash of gold freckles on Phaedra's cheek.

"I can stay here with you. All I want to do… all I've ever wanted to do was take care of you…. love you the way you love her."

Val leaned up and kissed Phaedra.

"Never asked you for that. I wanted you to love me the way *you* do. Just you. Not the makeup, or the hair, or the colorful eyes. I just wanted the quiet girl that held my hand after the last mastectomy. I wanted the woman that accepted me for who I was. The one I got on that plane for in the end."

"I never thought," Phaedra tilted her head and smiled.

"You never asked."

Phaedra sniffled as she pulled the blanket up onto Val's shoulder and huddled next to her.

"I've been a good wife. I've loved you better than anybody. You wanted loyalty so badly back then. Alana betrayed you by not coming to Paris. I stayed beside you, remember. She doesn't love you the way I do. You'd never leave me for her."

Val turned her face down into the pillow of her wife's breasts as she drifted in and out of unconsciousness.

"The cancer has spread throughout my entire body. I'm leaving you anyway, Phaedra."

* * *

It was a shot in the dark, but he had to try. Cass studied the Guggenheim Art Museum from his vantage point across the waterway. He marveled at the Golden Arcs. During the day, the marble took on a richer ancient feel. At night, it glowed a deep gold which seemed to echo the treasures inside.

Cass sat back against the tree, relishing the feel of the bark digging into his back. He took out a granola bar and studied the foil wrapper. Whenever he left the house for any long period of time, Alana would sit a bottle of water and a granola bar on the table next to the door.

During a heist Alana did the same thing. Her stakeouts of places took hours, and sometimes he'd catch a glimpse of her in the moonlight rocking back and forth ever so slightly, appearing to count the seconds.

At the oddest times she would rise to her feet and incline her ear. If she backed away, he knew the mission was scrapped. She wouldn't signal; she simply looked up at him and walked off. At first, he questioned, but then he would look back and see the guards had changed the rounds.

"Alana, if you're here, please walk away if you can. They're talking hard time now."

Cass jumped at the sound of his own voice in the dark. Alana never made a sound and trained their men not to either.

He sat up and peered across the water. The dark figure walking back and forth made Cass sit back against the tree and breathe a sigh of relief. It wouldn't happen tonight. He bit back a curse as the granola bar fell from his pocket onto the carpet of grass and leaves. He moved to search for it and very clearly his blood spoke.

"No sound."

As he made his way back to his car, he looked over his shoulder and a sweet, familiar pain tightened his chest.

* * *

Alana leaned against the tree studying his retreating figure as she popped a bit of the honey oat bar into her mouth.

CHAPTER 34

Three Weeks Later

Alana studied herself in the mirror. The dark circles around her eyes had a purple tint to them. The bruising around her midsection was gone, yet she ached. She ran her hand over her stomach then traced the bikini cut scar. She winced at the memory flooding her mind of Gabriel gripping her fingers when he nursed. She moved her hand to her nipple and gasped at the stab of pain she felt there. Alana stared at her reflection and backed away.

Val was standing in the door with her back turned holding her robe out to her.

"Phae says she's got an in at the Guggenheim."

Alana shrugged into the robe and tied it before turning to Val who was standing by her recliner.

"How are you feeling?"

Alana curved her hand around Val's hollow cheek. Val brushed her lips against her palm before she settled down in the chair. Alana eased herself down on the bed and studied her. Val was never a tall nor particularly strong woman. No matter how many tee shirts or sweatshirts she put on to conceal her shape, Val still looked frail. Now, looking at her head-on, she seemed smaller. The silk shirt she wore was unbuttoned low to give nurses access to the port stitched to her chest. Alana eased back the fabric and glanced at the bandage where the tubing should have been. Tears pricked her eyes as she took in the sad smile on Val's face.

"Last day of chemo… by choice." Val buttoned her shirt then touched Alana's leg.

"After tonight, we have some easy days coming up. You and I have birthdays too. Phae's happy with the smash and grabs and the papers you've been finding, so she's got something planned. You gonna come through?

Alana chuckled.

"Haven't a thing to wear." She said with a look of mock annoyance.

Val nodded and put her head down.

"Don't worry about it; I got you."

Val gripped her arm as she rose unsteadily to her feet and shuffled to the door.

"I don't have the flu, Val. In fact, I haven't had a period since I got here. How long have you known?"

Val opened the door.

"Could have given you an abortion the second I knew. Couldn't stand the thought of you hating me anymore than you do."

"Val, I don't."

She turned, and Alana saw the runnel of blood coursing from Val's nose and the tears on her face.

"You should. She's making you wear a harness. You move too fast or too slow and she'll send a current through it, harmless to the babies, but it'll hurt like a son of a bitch to you."

Alana winced as the door closed.

She picked one of the dossiers on the nightstand and flipped it open.

The pages were filled with pictographs, glyphs, and snatches of foreign languages.

Alana turned the book around in her hands so that she was holding it right side up. She squinted at it as something on the edge of her memory whispered to her. Alana ran her hands over the script as she tried to form the words with her mouth, then suddenly her eyes flooded with recognition, and she slammed the book shut. Alana climbed from the bed, pulled on her leggings, and paced the room.

* * *

The Guggenheim security team was state of the art, but with the hackers and techno geeks on Phaedra's team the place still seemed ancient. Everyone had their roles and was busy executing them when she stepped into the vault.

Instead of blowing the vaults, Kanaan the head of Phaedra's technical team pressed a button on his laptop, and all the doors popped open.

Alana was halfway down the wall throwing files and strings of jewelry into the sports bag on the floor. She was searching for the glyph she'd seen earlier while rattling off in her head what they meant, when she felt it.

Her heart hammered in her chest as a fresh bout of adrenaline spiked from the top of her head down over her body. She felt her legs give out, and she hooked her arm into the safety deposit box. She pulled herself upright and turned around.

Cass was leaning in the doorway watching her with his muscular arms folded across his chest. She flattened herself against the wall as he moved forward, spinning the vault door closed. With every step he took he was closing the distance yet, in her mind, he was still a world away. He came to a stop, encasing her in his raw masculine heat.

"Cass…."

He took in a sharp breath and leaned into her.

"Shouldn't be here." She squeaked as she ran her tongue over her lips.

His gaze dropped to her lips, and he began to trace them with his fingers before he took her face in his hands and pulled her closer so that his mouth was against her ear. The heat of him was making her slide down the wall. He took a step closer, trapping her between his chest and the wall.

"We conceived our son in a vault just like this one."

"Cass, what are you doing here?"

He stepped back far enough to press his forehead against hers.

"I'm looking for my wife. Have you seen her?"

"Cass, you have to get…"

Alana wedged her hands between their chests and tried to push out. Cass hooked his hands under her arms and pinned her higher on the wall so that she had no choice but to wrap her legs around his hips.

"Can I have you…..I'll always ask… may I touch you?"

"Cass…"

He wasn't hearing her. His fingers traced the fine scar reaching back into her hairline. His lips trembled as he slowly surveyed her. He ran his thumb under her eye, and he blinked, revealing the exhaustion in his own eyes. When she tried to turn her face, he rested the side of his face in the space between her forehead and the tip of her nose.

"Can I…Hmm? Can I, have you?" he whispered before running his tongue down her neck and over her collarbone.

When he lifted his head, Alana took his face in her hands and kissed him hard and deep. His weight pushed her harder and higher against the wall as he covered her mouth with his own. Before she knew it, she'd reached between then and caressed the hot pulsing knot beneath his belt buckle. She pulled on the zipper, and he spilled into her hand. He yanked at the waistband of her leggings, pulling them down past her knees and filling his hands with her ass. Alana rocked her hips forward hard enough to drive him inside.

With every thrust she felt the hot, hard knob of him digging deeper and deeper. She closed her eyes as she buried her face in his neck. He shrugged her away from his shoulder and brought her mouth back to his, thrusting his tongue as hard as his hips.

Alana tried to return his kiss, but he dragged his open mouth across her cheek and down under her chin ending with a hard, sucking kiss to her pulse line. Each thrust put him deeper and forced a panting moan from her that he answered with a growl. She molded her body tighter to his as she matched his thrusts with ones of her own, each one harder than the last until the muscles in her thighs began to quiver, and she broke out in a light sweat.

Every nerve in her body hummed, drawing raw sexual energy from everywhere in her body into one bright pulsing charge that erupted, pulling her in all directions. She was exploding and imploding then freezing and melting. She looked deep into his eyes and watched as black fire rose in them and a cascade of molten hot tears from his soul glued them together. She turned her face into his shoulder and cried.

CHAPTER 35

Cass closed his eyes against the sobs that wracked her body. Alana never made a sound the rare times she did cry, and to hear the sounds emanating from somewhere deep made him crush her closer. He slipped her leggings back up over her hips and tried to absorb her sobs into his body.

He blinked at the tears blinding him as rage gave way to understanding and fear. She was sick. He could see that. The dark circles around her eyes and the cold clammy feel of her skin told him she was rapidly getting worse. He peeled her shirt back from her shoulder, giving him the agonizing answer to the question of the blood on her coat. He ran his thumb over the scar, and she cried harder and wrapped her legs tighter around his hips. He turned so that his back was against the wall and slid to the floor and just held her while he waited for the storm to pass.

The questions burning at the back of his throat seemed to crumble under her convulsive sobs, so much so that it was scaring him. He shrugged her away from his chest, and when she tried to lay back down against him he held her further away as he smoothed her hair back from her face and thumbed away a tear.

"Alana, what are you doing here?"

She ran the heel of her hand over her top lip.

"Gotta get you out of here. You can't be seen here."

"I won't be. I know how you work. Talk to me; this is a job isn't it. Somebody is making you. Answer me."

She chewed on her bottom lip.

"Hey, don't look at my chest. Look at me. Is this a job?"

When she summoned the courage to look at him, the grief and fatigue he saw there made him clutch her to his chest as her sobs returned.

"I couldn't stay with him, Cass. I left our son in the woods. He was crying for me, and I had to …. I had to leave him to keep him safe."

The words were on the tip of his tongue. *He's still crying, Alana. We all are.*

"He's fine. Monet is fine. They're smart. We trained them well."

Alana tore away from him and bounded to her feet.

"Have to finish this."

"Finish what? Talk to me dammit." He hissed as he gave her a sharp shake.

Alana gasped then went limp in his arms.

Cass swept an arm under her legs and sat back down. He dug into the side of her neck searching for a pulse and sighed when he found one. He was about to stand up when he felt a sharp jolt and a vibration jitter through Alana's clothing, making her cry out before she turned and threw up. Cass stuck his hand down the back of her shirt to feel the harness. The whiff of ozone. He clawed at the contraption.

Alana rolled off his lap and crawled over to the wall. She looked into the safety deposit box near her head and reached inside. Whatever she pulled out she stuck down the front of her shirt.

"Works better than a cattle prod. Stay here, Cass. Let me finish."

He grabbed her thigh and pulled her back onto his lap and smoothed her hair out of her face.

"Fuck that. What you need to do is come home with me before you get killed."

"And if I do that before giving Phaedra what she wants she'll kill you all. And if that happens, I'm dead anyway." Her gaze dropped to the stain on his shirt, and her eyes flooded with tears.

"Oh my God, I threw up…. My waste is all over us. Have to get clean."

"Stop it. For the last time you are not dirty. Stop it!"

Cass clutched her back to his chest and tried again to absorb the tremors whip cording through her body. She flinched again and again, crying out with each jolt.

He reached up her shirt to claw at the harness, and he felt the sharp stab of pain in his hand. Alana stilled his hand as she rolled onto her knees and pushed herself to her feet. She backed away from him until she was at the door.

"Give me a 20-minute head start. Get out of the vault and into the water in 3 minutes. Place is wired with Semtex."

Alana staggered to the door, spun the handle, and stumbled out into the dark.

CHAPTER 36

The french pressed coffee he choked down barely put dent in the exhaustion, but it was better than nothing. Cass finished the cup of coffee and ordered another. At this time of night very few of the outdoor cafés were open and even if they were, he wouldn't have gone to one. The whole alfresco concept was lost on him. Unless he was out at the stadium watching a football or baseball game, eating outside made little or no sense.

He took a sip of his coffee and surveyed the area. He'd spent the day at the hotel sitting with his back against his front door. He could still feel the heat of the blast pick him up and throw him into the water.

Alana.

Cass reached for the stain lost in his sodden clothes and massaged it. Every bit of venom, every argument, every plea had vanished when he felt the current ripple through her harness with a cruel zap. Seeing her, being with her had answered so many questions he didn't dare speak aloud. Her mouth against him, her sweet body clinging to his.

His children were right. Alana hadn't left him. She allowed herself to be taken… to save the children but most importantly to save him. Yet again. He downed more of the coffee, wishing for something stronger.

He pulled the laptop closer and keyed in Phaedra's name. Within seconds the search results filled the screen. Several media sources that announced a birthday party in honor of her wife.

Cass blinked away the memory and took another look around. The location was still clear. He was all set to settle in at the counter when he saw the faint glow of a lighter as a man lit his cigarette. Cass walked across the street and into the alley.

"Put your gun away, Garrett. If I wanted you dead, you wouldn't have much choice in the matter."

"I wouldn't be the only one," Cass said as he let the gun rest at his side.

"She's alive."

"Sorry, who are you…."

"I think we both know who I'm talking about, Garrett. Why else would you be in Rome? You planning on taking in the sights? Are you heading over to the National Roman Museum or the Vatican?"

"No, I don't know who you're referring to. Maybe I do plan on heading over to Vatican City."

"Please, your wife is the expert on fine art; you're nothing more than a boot, a lowly grunt like me following orders." Brian stepped from the shadows. "Yes, I am. I'm talking about your wife, Alana. I took a huge risk coming down here to meet you. Levine says you are a man to be trusted."

"I am."

"And that cuts zero grease with me right now. I've been immersed in this situation for most of my life. Turned my back on my sister for years. Now I'm entrenched, ready to betray the only family I've got, and for what, a lovesick husband?"

Cass tilted his head and looked at the man. "Maybe you need to ask yourself a question. I heard about Knox. I saw the body. You were agency long before you started moonlighting. Name an agency rule that matches up with the murder of an old man."

"The gunshot wound was self-inflicted."

"Did he tie himself to the chair as well?"

Brian ran a hand over his face and started to walk away. "I cut the rope before I left. Look, things got out of control. If I'd stepped in..." His voice trailed off. "The man did his dirt; wasn't like he was an innocent."

"And that makes it all okay? Did you beat him, or did you watch?"

"Look, it's gonna haunt me the rest of my days. He didn't know anything anyway, even after Alana spoke to him. Your wife has nerves of steel. She can handle her shit."

Cass stared at him, aghast. "So, you bring my wife into this to what, cover your tracks? You plan on throwing my wife under the bus once she out lives her usefulness?"

"You really have no idea who you're dealing with, do you?"

"You know what? I'm tired of people thinking that with enough money and power they can do anything they want."

"Phaedra Khalid and Valerie Banks are dangerous."

"So I keep hearing."

"Val's not your problem. Phaedra is. My sister won't let anything happen to Alana. Val was livid when she found out Alana was hurt in that car accident. We followed her from the store out onto the road leading into the woods."

"You pushed my wife into that river?" Cass moved closer to the man.

"We never counted on Alana outmaneuvering us. When we brought her in, she was hurt bad, but Val took over her care. Alana isn't fighting her that's for sure."

"What are you talking about?"

"Look, maybe you need to just head home and let things play out. Levine clued me in on some of Alana's history. Phaedra and Val were her people long before you. Maybe she just wanted to come home"

"Her home is with me and her children."

Brian shrugged deeper into his coat.

"So you say. Come on. I don't like being exposed like this."

Brian turned to walk away then came back. "You're about my size. Come on, I have a tux you can put on."

CHAPTER 37

The music pulsated through the ballroom. Bodies of all shapes, sizes, and colors twisted and writhed in time with the bass that made the floor and the windows of the grand ballroom vibrate. Lights flashed and flickered in time with a DJ that constantly worried the amplifier and other equipment that surrounded him.

Val swirled the green absinthe in a skull-shaped goblet. The white sugar cubes sitting in the bowl reminded her of teeth. Sometimes she liked the Louche, the opaque liquid that the sugar and fennel made when combined with ice cold water. But tonight she wanted to skip the pleasantries and go straight for the gut. Absinthe never failed when the pain got so bad she felt like screaming. She glanced around at the dimness and smiled. Phaedra made sure to keep the lights as dim as possible over Val's table. The candle sitting on the table gave off just enough light to make it seem like a cave.

People stopped by her table, offering birthday greetings before tossing some unwanted gift on a steadily growing pile. Some people skipped the pleasantries and dropped their gift on the pile as if it were some sort of cover charge. From where Val sat, she could see Phaedra with her blonde braids shimmering like spun gold moving from one group of people to another. Her laughter was like clear crystal, distinct above the roar of the bone-crunching thump of the bass.

Brian slid into the end of the booth closest to Val. "Phaedra wanted me to tell you that if you were feeling poorly, I could take you back to the Presidential suite. She's got your doctors on standby and an ambulance in the parking lot."

Val let her head roll across the cushion she had been resting against until she was looking at him. She ran her warm honey-brown hand under her nose and swallowed hard at the gorge that kept rising in her throat. "Phaedra knew I was feeling poorly before we left the suite. Let her finish her networking session, because this damn sure isn't a party."

Brian shook out one of the napkins on the table and pushed it into Val's hand. "How'd we get mixed up in this, Val? We're the peppercorns in a fucking salt bin. In another life, you and Phaedra wouldn't even run in the same circles. She looks like she could be some country club owner's trophy wife passing for white, not that those skin treatments are making her any lighter. And us... put us in suits but we still look like street."

She closed her eyes and let the bass and her personal green goblin whipcord through her.

"You haven't touched any of the drinks people sent to you."

Val opened her eyes and looked around as if she had been sleeping. She glanced down at her empty skull-shaped shot glass being dwarfed by the matching goblet and smiled. "If I want to be polite, I drink Ketel One. Everclear, if I'm in a killing mood. These days I'm finding that I can't stomach either."

"So, what's this?" Brian took the glass and sniffed the contents, and his eyes widened. "Smells like licorice. Do you know what absinthe will do to your insides?"

"Your government salary is a mere pittance compared to the ridiculous amount I pay you. Stay out of my glass." Val leaned forward and plucked the glass from the table and held it out to him before throwing back the last of the drink. She fell back against the pillow and closed her eyes. "Besides, the cancer has eaten away everything else. How much damage could it really cause? Did you bring him?"

Brian shot a look at Val as she poured another shot of absinthe over the sugar cubes. "I left him in the room. Why don't you just let me kill him?"

Val snapped her head in his direction and moved to say something then stopped. "Alana never asks for anything, and tonight is her birthday too. Just... give her some space. Phaedra thinks I brought him here to torture Alana. Whatever works, right?"

Val nodded once as she settled back in her chair.

Alana walked into the room flanked by two guards. Val put both of her hands on the table as she pushed further up on the chair. The slight pause in the conversation was enough to make Phaedra turn around. She excused herself from her conversation and came over to the table where Val was sitting.

"She's all you ever wanted... well, here you go. Happy Birthday."

"Don't put her in the middle of this, Phaedra." Val warned.

"She's always been between us, your precious idol, Alana. You were half dead when we pulled you off the tarmac that night.... crying in your sleep like a little bitch for her after your mastectomies.... called out for her more than once when we fucked. You worship at her feet."

"And this is supposed to make me love you more, Phaedra? In front of all these people, you're gonna do this?"

"Oh no lover, this is all about networking. You see, I found out where another stone is located. Alana is going to make nice with a certain guest to go get it. Told you I had an 'in'; I just thought you'd like to watch. You used to love watching, remember, darling?"

* * *

Alana made her way to the table. She was dressed in an off-white form-fitting gown, and her hair was pinned up ornately with combs that glittered with diamonds.

It never even occurred to her to protest.

When Alana woke up and looked around the room, all she saw was Brian and a woman clutching a cosmetics bag to her chest.

"Untie her," he said quietly.

The woman sat her bag down and started working at the cloth tethers on Alana's wrist. Alana lay perfectly still as she studied the woman. She let her eyes slip shut when she heard the distinct click of the safety being removed from a gun.

"If you do anything other than sit up and open the box at the foot of the bed, I won't kill you. I'll just kill this nice lady here, and I know you don't want any more blood on your hands."

"I didn't kill your father, Brian."

The woman shied away, falling back against the wall as Alana sat up slowly.

"No, you just shamed him. Everybody in the neighborhood knew what he was doing because of you. I mean, how did you get into the church service with that tape?"

"Everyone in the neighborhood knew what he was doing, because he hurt other children in that neighborhood, too. Your father killed himself. I didn't put the gun in his hand. Now, where's the envelope?"

"What?"

"Phaedra always has an envelope with my instructions."

"Not tonight. It's Val's birthday. Val had this shipped from a dressmaker in Milan. She also sent those blue lilies over there. She said you two shared the same birthday. Clean yourself up and put this on."

Alana snapped back to reality at the feel of Val's cold, skeletal hand encircling hers as she pulled her over to sit beside her. "Hey, Val," she whispered.

Val turned Alana's hand over and ran her thumb over the raw IV site. "Why didn't you let the nurse take this out the right way?" Alana tried to pull her hand away, but Val tightened her grip.

"Wouldn't matter if I did. Phaedra summoned me. Ordered Brian to kill an innocent if I did anything but sit up and open the box you left on the end of my bed. Thanks for the flowers by the way. The peg is here. I won't sleep with him. I love my husband and my children too much to..."

Val gripped Alana's wrist harder. "I'd never ask you to do that."

"But she will, and what do you think I should do? For the safety of my children and my husband, what should I do? After all, you two just love to be entertained. What's the saying, once a whore always a whore?"

"Alana, I never thought that about you. Never," Val whispered.

Just then Phaedra came over to the table. "Well it looks like you two are getting along famously. Alana, I want you to meet a friend of mine. Rob Englund, this is Alana Symone. He saw you across the room, and he was captivated."

Alana looked up into the man's face to see his eyes crawling over her. He lifted her hand and pressed his cold, greasy lips to the back. He looked back at Phaedra, and then tugged at Alana's hand.

"Come dance with me; let's get to know each other better."

Val tightened her grip on Alana's hand. Alana could see the silent war raging between the two women. Alana pulled her hand from the man and rested it on top of Val's. Val turned and looked at her, shaking her head no. Alana patted Val's hand before gently peeling her fingers from her wrist.

"Happy birthday, Val," Alana whispered before the man grabbed her hand once more and all but dragged her from the booth.

CHAPTER 38

"I still think this is a bad idea."

Cass looked over at Brian who watched him fasten the snaps on the Glock pistol he was securing under his tuxedo jacket.

"My wife wants to come home."

"Really?" Brian folded his arms across his chest.

"You don't know my wife."

"I grew up with your wife and the trash pack of girls she ran with. Watched her wrap men around her finger. They'd kill or die for her. She killed my father."

"Alana never killed anybody."

"Did she think sending my sister out of town was gonna spare me? Every night Val was gone my father...you know what? She may not have pulled the trigger, but my father's blood is on her hands."

"Sounds like my wife did you a favor back when you were kids."

"You're no better than Phaedra, worshipping at the feet of someone who would just as soon leave you as stay with you. She's a liar, a thief.

I've watched her break into several banks over the last few days. She is as ruthless as they come. No, she doesn't hurt people, but something comes over her and whoever you may think she is doesn't exist."

"Never said my wife wasn't focused." Cass shrugged deeper into his tuxedo jacket. "I've seen her stand toe to toe with some of the worst pimps in Shadow Bay as she fought for some of those girls. Saw her on a few heists myself. I know what my wife is."

"You sound almost proud of her."

A faint smile touched Cass' features as he buttoned his jacket. "I am. She stood in the gap for me and for countless others. She scares the hell out of me sometimes, but, yeah, I am proud. She has survived so much, and I know my wife isn't afraid to die."

"That's not a smart way to live. Phaedra and Val know what you look like. What do you think you're going to accomplish by doing this?"

Cass shook his head. "You're missing the point. My wife stood up and took two cop killer rounds for me. Just stood up. You've seen how small my wife is. She apologized to me because she thought she had failed. At the time I thought she was a stranger, but low and behold I discovered she is so much more. No, my wife's periscope is higher than everybody's, and she will do whatever she has to do to keep me and our children safe. I just want her to know she isn't alone in all of this. I'm not going to lose her to this."

"You love her that much?"

"I was willing to die with her once. I'll do it again if I have to."

"So, what's your plan? Do you intend to shoot it out for her?"

"If it comes to that, yeah. But I think Phaedra wants to be entertained. From what I've read and what I see now, she likes throwing grenades into people's lives just so that she can sit somewhere and watch. I know the type. I think she wants to degrade my wife for some reason. For all I know, maybe she plans to use me for that purpose."

"Again, what's your plan? You gonna walk in there?"

"I won't have to. Once I'm there, my wife will come to me."

"You really believe that shit? Christ, we're all dead then. Look, stay in this room. I'll bring her to you."

* * *

Alana winced at the man holding her close. He stank of too much cologne. His hands crawled all over her. At one point his hand reached her ribs and she stiffened against him. He pulled back and studied her face. He ground his hips into her.

"It's okay baby. I feel it, too. All you have to do is make nice, and Daddy will give you a prize." He leaned in and ran his tongue just beneath her ear.

Alana jerked away from the man and fell to her knees.

"Gabe told me once that you were never late."

Ice water washed down Alana's spine. It couldn't be. Cass was supposed to be back in the States with Monet and Gabriel. He was safe. He was...she sat down hard, refusing to look up at either of them.

"No, she's my date. Find your own."

"It's obvious she doesn't want to be anywhere near you. Leave her to me and I won't break your fucking arm."

Cass' voice was as welcome as rain across cracked earth, but Alana still refused to look up, refused to believe he was there. He was supposed to be home. The kids needed him there. She felt like she was losing her mind. She had to be. She closed her eyes and shook her head. She didn't know if mental illness ran in her family, but it almost seemed like poetic justice for all the crimes she had committed.

It would be a welcome relief to detach from the world and slip away into madness. She could live on hallucinations. She could lose herself in the memories of Cass and the children

At last she could finally slip away, even if only in her mind. Her body could remain here, but she didn't have to. It was another tool Isla had placed in Alana's war chest; a tool that would help her survive. It served her when the johns did things to make her scream, and again when Julian wanted to exercise his husbandly rights. It wouldn't matter. None of it would matter because Cass was with her. She could go off in her head and he would be there, waiting in their bedroom, waiting to hold her... waiting to...

"Dance?"

Cass interrupted her thoughts. The warmth of his breath bathed her shoulder as his lips came in contact with the side of her neck. Alana could feel it creak stiffly as she turned to look at him. She reached for his face then pulled back. "You're supposed to be home."

Cass caught her hand and kissed her palm and put it against his cheek. His midnight gaze glowed with savage fire. He smoothed an errant lock of her hair back from her face. "Dance with me, Alana."

Alana felt his arm slip around her waist as he stood up, bringing her to her feet. He clutched her to his chest and laced her fingers with his own. Leaning against him for a moment, she tried to regain her strength. She felt her legs give out once more, and the arm around her waist tightened enough for her to regain her footing. She rested her face against the taut smoothness of his shoulder as a jazzy version of 'As if We Never Met' played in the background.

"First time I danced with you, I felt like I couldn't hold you close enough."

"Cass," she breathed.

"You were like quicksilver in my hands. The tighter I held you, the faster you slipped through my fingers. Just like now."

"Cassiel, you can't be here. You have to..."

He leaned back enough to look at her. "What, let you go?"

"Shouldn't be here."

He yanked her closer making her gasp. He turned his face down against her ear. "And neither should you."

"You have to go... you have to get out of here."

"And you can't stay, Alana. Do you really think these people are going to let me out of here now?"

* * *

Phaedra flopped down in the chair beside Val. Val let her gaze drift from Alana and Cass to Phaedra.

"You never held me like that. Not even once." Phaedra looked over at

Val and handed her a clean linen napkin.

"As I recall, you weren't the touchy-feely type, remember? Made me clean my hands every time I touched you in the beginning, like I was dirty or something." Val tossed back another shot of absinth as she watched Cass rest his face against Alana's.

"You brought him here for her, didn't you?" Phaedra waved her hand to summon one of her guards.

Val's hand snaked out and gripped Phaedra's wrist. "It's our birthday, mine and hers, remember? I can have anything I want, and so can she."

Phaedra turned in her seat to look at Val. The bemused look on her face made Phaedra seethe. "Embarrassing me in front of our friends. This is what you want?" she asked.

The sheen of tears in Phaedra's eyes made Val loosen her grip on Phaedra's wrist. Val reached for her face, then ran the back of her hand against Phaedra's cheek.

"Correction, *your* friends. And besides, you always said you liked to be entertained." Phaedra turned back to the crowd to see Cass take Alana by the hand and walk toward the exit. She stood, and Val gripped her wrist again. "You're going to let the last chance of us getting the stones just walk out the door?" Phaedra moved to summon her guard once more.

"We have people in the States watching her family. All it would take is a phone call. She won't go far."

Phaedra looked back at Val and sat back down. "You trust her that much?"

Val shrugged. "So did you a long time ago. She got you out of the sewers, out of a lot of impossible places. I know of one in particular."

"I didn't ask her for that."

"Even after you dispatched me and some other kids to beat the shit out of her, she still got you out of there. Nobody else could. Julian damn sure didn't."

"That was once, Val." Phaedra interrupted.

"And look at us now." Val waved a hand dismissively. "She did all the dirty work, got dumped on, and for what? Us? Were we even worth it?

I remember how you always used her last name, as if she didn't deserve to be called by her first name. She was bitch or ho, anything but her name. Never Alana. I remember how you accused her of being a taker, knowing damn well that girl gave more… saved more of us. And you accused her of being a taker."

"How can you say that? Look at what we've built."

"People stand on the backs of geniuses all the time to get what they want. What we do doesn't require a whole lot of talent, Phaedra, but Alana… even you must admit she's more than a genius. Smarter than you and better than me."

"We have to kill him. You know that. She won't come back. She'll hate you. Can you live with that?"

Val sat up and leaned on the table. "She doesn't hate either one of us, Phaedra. After everything we've done to her, we deserve her hatred and more, but she doesn't hate us."

"So, we let her go?"

Val downed another shot of absinthe and settled back against the cushions once more. "She loves him enough. She'll break any vow or promise she's made to him to keep him alive. She won't stay with him. She can't."

"Can you live with your competition fucking her?" Phaedra spat.

Val let her eyes slip shut. "It's my birthday, Phaedra. I can have whatever I want, right?"

"Yeah."

"Then shut the fuck up."

CHAPTER 39

Alana struggled in the viselike grip Cass had on her hand. His grip wasn't painful, but she knew he had no plans of stopping. Alana looked back toward the ballroom. No one had come after them.

Cass gunned the ignition and sped out of the parking lot. Once they were back in his hotel room he threw his keys on the nightstand. Alana stepped away from his hard, tense body as she warily looked around the room.

"You shouldn't be here."

"Neither should you."

"And what would you have me do, Cassiel? Come home? Maybe next time we don't find Monet. Maybe I can't get our son to safety, then what?" Alana began to cry. She scraped at her face, disgusted at the sight of her own tears. "Or maybe...maybe I just come home to find you in your shop with a bullet in your head? I'm sorry, Cass, but I can't live with that. I can't. Believe what you want, Cass. I can't fight you. I have no pride where you're concerned. All I know is that I love you and maybe I shouldn't. Call me silly, but after all these years, you asking if you can have me still matters more than anything."

"Alana." He reached for her, and she backed away from him.

"I asked for this and now...just go. My past is alive and well. I'll never live it down. I did what I had to because no one gave a damn about what I wanted. You want to know what my biggest crime was? It wasn't the heists or the jewels or the drugs I carried, the money or even the tricks. My sin is that I had the audacity to survive, and I will pay for that crime for the rest of my life. Twice I paid for your life with mine, and it's still not enough, not even for you. I betrayed untold numbers of people because you needed me to. You asked me to trust you, and I did, knowing that this day would come. Deep down inside, knowing that even the man I once gave my soul to would question my motives. This is where I belong; back where I started with people who know me better than you ever could. Get out of here."

Cass dragged Alana into his arms. "No, you don't get to dismiss me like some wayward child. "

Alana twisted and struggled in his arms. "Let me go!"

Cass covered her mouth with his. His kiss was punishing, angry. Alana felt her legs give out. Cass swept his arm under her legs and carried her to the bed. His fingers trembled as he unzipped her gown and eased the lacy cup of her bra aside. His touch was light and painfully teasing as his hand slipped between her thighs to massage her. "Nobody leaves, remember?" he whispered as he devoured her mouth once more.

With each gentle stroke, he moved her dress further and further up her thighs. Finally, he guided her up to his chest and pulled the dress over her head. Alana grabbed his clothing, pushing and pulling at them until he was gloriously naked above her. She writhed beneath him as his gaze swept over her.

"Say it," he growled, making her shudder as he lapped at the skin just beneath her left ear.

"Cassiel, please," she whispered.

He sat back and looked at her. "No. Say it."

"Nobody leaves."

"Say it again, Alana. Again."

"Nobody leaves."

She took his face in her hands and shook him once, making him look at her.

"Can I have you, Cass?"

"You've always had me, Alana."

He let his hands explore the soft lines of her back, her waist, and her hips. Every place his hands fell he traced with his open mouth before he positioned her under him. Slowly he moved his hands downward to lift her thighs over his hips and drove himself deep inside her. Alana cried out against his shoulder and matched his thrusts with her own. The pleasure was pure and explosive; waves of ecstasy throbbed through them. The more he filled her, the more she wanted of him. With every thrust he was shattering the hard shell she had built so carefully around her soul. The heat of him was intoxicating. His sweat rained down on her and fire spread through her heart as he moaned her name repeatedly.

His hardness electrified her as he gently turned her over and entered her from behind. She recognized the flush of raw sexual desire she hadn't felt in months, and molten hot pleasure rippled under her skin. Her heart burst with love and anguish because she knew it couldn't last, and as his passion inched through her veins she turned to him and clutched at his hips, hypnotized by the urgent pressure of his mouth against her nipple. It was too much to hope for and all that she wanted to live for. The turbulence of his passion continued to surround her, and she knew she had to survive this ordeal, not simply for her children, but for Cass. Alana rose to meet Cass in a moment of uncontrolled passion, and as his body tensed with release, Alana felt the electric shock of her own course through her body, forcing another orgasm from him.

When she came around, he was clutching her to his chest. She reached up and erased the tears on his face. He quickly captured her hand in his and kissed the back of it. Alana caught the glint of her rings hanging from Monet's necklace that he'd laced through her fingers.

"I never asked for that necklace or my rings back."

She turned her face into his chest, curled up into a fetal position against him and sobbed.

He held her and waited for her storm of tears to quiet. She ran a finger over the scar on his chest, then sat up against him. She raked her hand through her hair and began to shake her head.

"Cassiel, I can't accept these." She tried to pull the rings from her hand, and he stopped her.

"Stop it. What are you doing?" Cass set her away from him. He shook her gently, and she opened her eyes. She traced the scar on his cheek.

"Please try to understand. They allowed this... it was part of the bargain."

"I traveled clear across this world to bring those rings to you... to bring you home. You're safe now. I'll call Nicholas and we'll go home."

"What? No... no, you have to leave me here. I meant what I said. I have to finish this."

"No, I don't."

Cass shook Alana again, and she blinked slowly while studying the room around them. "They allowed this... they plan to keep you. Oh my God, what have I done? No, you've got to get out of here. I asked her for this.... they saw you at the party. They know you're here. They won't let you go now."

"I don't give a damn who saw me. I walked into that fucking party to find you. I'm not leaving here without you. They'll have to kill me first."

"I give a damn. I cannot lose you; do you hear me? I can't!" She jerked away from him and got up.

"Whatever you've done. Whatever you're doing, they won't give you a year in prison this time, Alana."

"What else is new, Cassiel? The threat of hard time has been over my head since I first walked the streets. Maybe inside I can finally get some sleep. Maybe inside I can finally sit still."

Cass gripped her arm and made her face him.

"You are *not* staying here."

"And if I do go with you, then what? Teach Alana another lesson in what happens when she disobeys. Isn't that right, Cop? How long will I sit in an interrogation room this time? How long will I have to dance my little dance? How will I pay for my freedom this time: on my back or my knees? Let go of me, Cop." She looked down at his hand on her arm and then back up at him. She straightened her back with an air of defiance.

"What...? You haven't called me that in years."

"Because you haven't acted like one in years. Suspicious of my every move. Scratch a liar, find a thief. Isn't that right, Cop?" she shoved at him as hard as she could, but he barely stepped back from her.

"Stop calling me that. You did lie to me in the beginning. You lied by omission just recently. I asked you point blank."

"Couldn't tell you what I didn't know, Cass."

"And what about Stacey, huh? What about the girl at the restaurant? Whatever she told you cost that girl her life."

"What? What are you...?" Alana blinked as if he'd slapped her. "No... that's not... Stacey was upset with me because I put vice on the warehouse where they were using her and some other girls for skin flicks. She saw herself as an actress. All I saw was a fourteen-year-old girl being used up by Phaedra Khalid's subsidiaries." She found her gown and turned her back to pull it on.

"I'm sorry, Alana, I just assumed."

"You always *assumed* when it came to me. Always knew what was best. Always knew the answers." She smoothed down her dress and worked at fixing her hair. Behind her she could hear the rustle of fabric when he pulled on his pants. She scraped her sleeve over her cheek, once again leaving a red hash mark. "Why are you here? It's obvious how you got in, but why? You had to know..."

"Why am I here?" He walked across the room and snatched her up and shook her. "You can fix your face to ask me that?" He dropped her and backed away a step. "Our son is screaming in his sleep, but that's only when he can sleep. Monet stopped eating, so Myra resorted to force feeding her."

"Unimportant." She muttered.

Cass yanked her back around to face him.

"Seriously. I tell you our kids are dying without you. I'm here trying to save our lives, and it's all 'unimportant'."

"Funny, so am I. Go back to the children, and they'll be safe."

"Not all of them," he said quietly.

"What?" Alana backed away from him.

Cass walked her over to the bed then took a step closer, and she lost her balance and sat down. He knelt before her. "How far along are you?"

* * *

"Cassiel, I can't…"

"I asked you a question. Hmm?" he grabbed her hips and pulled her forward. "I noticed it in the vault. Your hair seems longer, your breasts are bigger, and you're softer in places. You carry towards your back. Even your scent... you smell sweeter."

"Maybe it's not yours. Maybe I am the whore you think I am."

He glared at her, and she stopped talking. "Stop it. My scent is all over you. You had that same smell when you carried Gabe. Stop trying to make me hate you."

"If it keeps you alive then maybe you need to. Please do this for me." A strangled sob leapt from her throat, and she pressed her face against his.

Cass kissed away her tears before he stood up, lifting her with him. He wordlessly unzipped her gown, and she let it fall back to the floor. He placed his hand on her midsection, and she stepped back enough to move his hand over to her right side.

"Your son," she said softly, moving his hand over to her left side. "Your daughter."

Just then, they both heard voices outside. Alana pulled away and slipped the gown back on. She peered out the window, then came back over to him; she pulled her rings off and pushed them into his hand.

"No..."

"Give them to someone that deserves them. You're free now, Cass. I will send the babies when I can. Tell our children I loved them."

She moved to step away, but Cass grabbed her from behind and held her. "Alana, no. I won't let you do this."

"Cassiel, please. If they find you here…what about the children? They won't stop; I know they won't. They'll kill Mark and Myra... please, Cass, please go back to them."

Alana pulled away and managed to get the door open. Val's gunmen flooded the room with their guns drawn. Alana moved back in front of Cass. He sidestepped her and moved her behind him.

"She's right, you know." Val's voice was so soft that at first Cass wasn't sure he'd heard anything.

"My guards will kill you and your people in the States if you don't let her walk out of here."

"Val, wait." Alana tried to move past Cass, but he forced her to stand still.

"Do as I say, Alana. He won't be harmed. You have my word. But if he keeps this up, Phaedra will come in here. She has no qualms about killing this man right in front of your eyes."

Alana jerked away from Cass, stiffened her back, and walked out the door.

"Get dressed," Val called back into the room.

CHAPTER 40

"You don't remember me, do you?"

"Should I?" Cass watched Alana head to the waiting limo.

"Your twin would remember me better. Father Gabriel was always trying to get me to come in and get fed or talk to the social workers. When I wasn't trying to boost his old sedan, I was fixing it."

Cass emerged from the room with his head tilted, taking in the small woman. He squinted as he searched the shadows and swirls of cigarillo smoke that surrounded her face. Out of the corner of his eye, he saw Brian move his hand to his gun.

"Take her home," Val called over her shoulder.

"Phaedra said not to leave your side," another guard said feebly.

"My name is on the bottom of your check. Don't miss your paper because you forgot who your real boss is." Val's eyes never left Cass' face as she spoke. She took another slow drag from her smoke.

"What if he tries to...?" the man moved closer to Val.

"He won't. He loves his wife too much. Now get out of here or I'll gut you myself."

"Alana could get me to do anything. Talk, eat, even betray her in the end. She is the only person on this planet I would allow to slap me hard enough to make my nose bleed and forgive her anyway."

"I don't..." He shook his head slightly.

"Don't matter. After you get passed around the entire male side of your family like a blunt, what is there really to say?"

He watched something that resembled a smile whisper across her gaunt face.

"Everybody called me Chatter, not that I talked much. Gave up that nickname with my left breast. Name's Val."

"Where are they taking Alana? Just give her to me."

"She shouldn't be out here in the cold." Val shrugged deeper into her black leather bomber jacket.

"She has no business here at all, Chat... Val. She should be home."

"Alana *is* home."

"With people who love her."

"She has that, too."

"With her husband and her children."

"If she does what she's been asked to do..."

Cass cut her off. "It won't be like the last time. If law enforcement catches up with her, they intend to put her away for a long time. She can't deal with that again."

"You mean *you* can't." Val took another drag on her cigarillo and exhaled slowly. "Alana won't see a day in prison."

"She already has, and it damn near killed her."

"She wouldn't have gone to prison if you'd let her finish whatever it was Julian laid out for her to do."

Cass walked past her and out into the light. "You don't really believe that if you knew anything about Julian Barlow. He was going to kill her... tried to."

"You know Alana came to me in the hospital when they kept shooting me up with poison to kill the tumors? Every single time I needed Alana, she was there."

"What does any of that have to do with it? You mean this is all your doing?"

"I played my role." Val lowered herself to the bench in the center of the courtyard.

"It's our birthday. Did you know that? You know what she asked for? Not freedom, not that my wife would give it to her anyway. Alana asked for you. Her loving you just now was my gift to her, and her way of saying goodbye."

Cass stood in front of her with his arms folded. "What kind of friend...?"

"Don't get it twisted. We go way beyond that. She won't be harmed if you stay in your lane." Val took another drag, and she turned to look at him full on. "Just leave my family alone."

"The way you looked at her just now wasn't exactly like family. You looked like a jealous lover. You angry she made love to me?"

"Save the reverse psychology, Garrett. You're not good at it, and besides, I told my men to bring you here because *she* needed you. I also told them not to kill you. I never said that *I* wouldn't."

"She was happy. She has a family that loves her."

"So do I!" Val hissed. "And if you don't leave her right where she is, then Phaedra will kill her. Or worse, Phaedra will just kill you in front of her. Can you live with that because I can't?"

"You brought her to this. Why would you throw in with a monster like Phaedra?"

"For the same reason you threw in with Alana. That's supposed to be my birthday party back there, but it doesn't even matter if I'm in that room. Phaedra is the life of the party. The camera, the attention, it's always on her. Underneath it all, my wife is very insecure, very vulnerable. She's been through a lot too. Alana wasn't Julian Barlow's only victim."

"What does that have to do with anything?"

"Shut up and listen. You ever meet a person and feel like they had the world handed to them when others needed it more? That's Phaedra. She and Alana were no different, but people were drawn to Alana, still are.

My wife is a social moth, and Alana is the fucking inferno."

"Whatever it is you think she has or knows. Let me take her home."

"There are people already in the states ready to take your children and kill your best friend and his family if you so much as try. Let Alana finish whatever it is Phaedra has her doing."

"Even if it kills her?"

"I won't let that happen. I've been the buffer between them for this long."

"And I'm supposed to trust you? You don't exactly look real healthy right now."

"Then Alana doesn't have much time, does she?"

CHAPTER 41

Six weeks later.

Bouncing around in a hot jeep did little to make her stomach settle. Val gave her crackers and ginger ale on the plane, but nothing she ate stayed down. Val almost envied Alana as she folded herself around her unborn children. It looked like someone had turned on a light under Alana's tissue paper soft skin. Alana was always beautiful to her, but now, with new life growing inside of her, she was even more so. Alana was starting to show, just enough to make her look softer. But while her skin glowed with new life, Alana's green eyes had lost their sparkle. It had been weeks since she last saw her husband, and it showed.

Alana managed to get another stone from a vault in some oil magnate's bedroom while Phaedra delighted the man with her easy banter downstairs at dinner. Now there was only one stone left. Alana had been the key piece in finding it. The paper that she'd pulled from the vault in Paris made little or no sense to Phaedra and her interpreters, and for the longest time, Alana sat back and watched them try to figure it out. Val was proud of her. Alana had them send her off on a snipe hunt for weeks, knowing full well they would turn up nothing. Then finally at dinner one night, Alana looked over at Val and straightened her back.

"Museum Island and the Kells washed out; The Walters in the States can't possibly house the stones. The only other place it could be is back in Somalia. Isla returned home many times. There is a mining facility. We'll find all the diamonds and conflict minerals you could possibly want. From what I've read, we'll need to get to the marketplace in Sierra Leone... anywhere on the Ivory Coast. The papers suggest that beneath one of the ruins, Wargaade Wall, there is an extensive refinery that takes the conflict diamonds and minerals and prepares them for the world market."

Phaedra moved her chair closer as she studied the photos of the ancient text. "How do I know you aren't lying about this? You've been studying these pictures for weeks. We've had scholars come in and try to decipher it, and now suddenly you know something."

Alana sat back slowly, making a conscious effort not to rub her stomach in front of Phaedra.

"You know I could cut those babies out of you if you lied to me, don't you? Maybe I'll let you carry them to term and kill you then... turn them out when they come of age."

Alana took in a slow breath as a faint smile whispered across her features. "Before or after you get your precious diamond? Where is my husband? What have you done with him?"

"I told you. He's dead." Phaedra glanced at Val.

Val reached across the table to grab Alana's hand, and Alana pulled away.

"Who's lying now? I would know if he were dead. Why is it I can still feel him moving through my blood?"

"Alana, stop... okay?" Val said quietly.

"Where is he, Val?" Alana let her gaze shift to Val.

They both watched as Phaedra rose to her feet and called for one of the guards. "Find my assistant. We'll need passage for the three of us to Somalia."

"Two. You already had a bout of malaria that almost took you away from here, Phaedra. I'll go." Val stared at Alana.

"You could get sick, too."

"I'm not sick Phaedra, I'm dying."

"No."

"Either I go alone, or she doesn't." Val sat back and downed a shot of Ketel One from her shot glass.

Phaedra moved to protest, but one look from Val and she shook her head and walked out.

* * *

They hit another bump, which jarred Val out of her thoughts and sent a vicious wave of nausea through her. She leaned her head out the window as she quietly got sick. When she leaned back in, Alana was awake watching her in the dim light. Alana held out a handkerchief and gestured slightly with her head. Val took the cloth and wiped her mouth before she pressed it under her nose.

"You should be resting, Val. You're in the end stages now. I'd give you a blood transfusion, but you might bleed out and make it worse."

"And I wouldn't let you. You're not spare parts for anybody. Certainly not me." She swabbed at her nose then rolled her eyes. "Besides, here or in hospice, I'm still dying. Here's better. I saw France and Greece. Always wanted to go to both places when I was a little girl. Wanted to go to college abroad, but someone had to stay. Mom was already gone and Brian... I couldn't leave him there, no matter how much he worshipped my father."

Val rested her hand on Alana's stomach. Alana covered Val's hand with her own. "Let me get you to a hospital, or at least let me get a doctor, Val. I know you're in pain."

"After everything Phaedra and I have done to you...Why?"

Alana looked out at the terrain for a long time.

"Even after I helped beat you to shit." Val leaned over and nudged her. "Tell me why, Alana."

"It's the only thing I was ever really good at, besides stealing. Call it my blind spot if you will. Couldn't change what was happening to me, but I could be the buffer."

"I'm the buffer between you and Phaedra. She was mad as shit, but I had to come, Alana. Guess I'm her blind spot. Phaedra would never deny me. It was always peaceful with you. The quiet. Phaedra needs the noise, craves it like crack. Always on, always ready to be the center of attention. I was content to have a book in my hands and some music playing in the background."

"Why did you marry her?"

"Thought you were dead. Felt like I'd been gutted and left to bleed out. Phaedra needed someone to take care of her, and I guess I needed to take care of somebody, too. When I found out you were alive, I tried to hate you for not coming home, but I couldn't. So, I married Phaedra."

"Do you love her?"

Val looked out at the lush terrain.

"I married her."

"But do you *love* her?"

Val turned her face up to the sun. The heat was stifling, yet there was an earthy scent to the air that made her smile. At last, she opened her eyes and looked at Alana.

"I gave her my name, Alana."

* * *

Alana watched as Val slipped in and out of consciousness. At any point on the drive over she could have jumped from the jeep and disappeared into the thicket. She glanced over at the man sitting in the front passenger seat polishing his machete. Every once in a while, he would cast a look back at her. Once, he'd gone so far as to stroke Alana's thigh with the handle of his machete. The man flinched when he felt Val dig the muzzle of her pearl handled Glock into his temple.

"Touch her again, and it will be the last thing you'll ever do."

CHAPTER 42

At the foot of the dead mountain range, people were walking back and forth with baskets. Some carried food while others carried what looked like mud. The first rays of sunlight had turned the sky the color of new bruises. Alana reached over to cover her with a blanket. Val opened her eyes and sat up. "You okay? Are the babies bothering you?"

Alana smiled at her old friend and smoothed a cool hand over her forehead. "We're fine. I'm concerned about you." She let her gaze drift from Val's face to the mountain range. "We are on blue ground, Val. We won't be safe here no matter who Phaedra thinks she knows. Yellow ground is up the mountain."

Val moved to sit up then thought better of it. "Give me a minute and I'll…"

"You won't survive the hike. Besides, from what I could gather from Isla's journal, she didn't hide the diamond here. Isla never set foot this far from Mogadishu. But if it's diamonds Phaedra wants." Alana raised a dismissive hand.

"I don't understand, you led us around on a goose chase all this time. What about Wargaade Wall? Why?"

"I needed to think. I needed to be sure my husband was alive, and he is. Isn't he, Val?"

Val gave her a wry smile and nodded. "He's too stubborn to die. Phaedra has him. He's her trump card. My people are in the States with your children, not to kill them, but to protect them if Phaedra can't rein herself in."

Alana chewed on her bottom lip for a moment, and then she relented. "Isla had children long before I came along. They died of starvation in the desert."

Val's eyes widened.

"Don't worry. We aren't going into the desert. Isla came back to Somalia lots of times. She had places where she stashed things."

"We've been to all of those places, Alana. Phaedra has everything your mother left behind for you."

"She can have it. I never wanted any of it, Val. I had what I wanted in the States. Cassiel, Gabriel, and Monet... now my twins. They are my treasures, Val."

"Gonna get you back to them." Val tried to sit up but fell back in the seat.

Alana fixed the blanket over Val's shoulder then smoothed a hand over her head. "They'll send a shipment of the blue and yellow ground deposits to Phaedra. The Kimberlite mines are vast here."

Val studied her. "What? How? You had no idea we were coming here."

"Someone saw me at the airport, and they got word here. My mother never set foot here, but her blood kin run this place. Phaedra's connection is really Isla's blood kin...my kin."

"The deposits are already on their way to France." A richly accented British voice washed over Alana's shoulder. The old man picked up Alana's hand and folded a stone into it. "For your friend. Some believe the dust of the diamond is a poison to be drunk by one's enemies, but the orange diamond holds the healing power of the Gods."

Val let her eyes drift to the old man standing there in an Italian suit as

Alana leaned forward and draped the amulet over Val's head. Val picked up the stone as the daylight continued to chase away the night.

The orange diamond picked up the rays of light making the stone glow with an inner fire.

"Where is the last diamond, Alana?" Val asked softly.

"Home."

"What?" Val dropped the amulet and inched up further in the seat.

"Isla came to visit me once in my prison cell. She told me that she took the diamond back where it all began. I thought she meant Mogadishu or Sierra Leone."

"I don't..."

"Isla was my mother. Knox was my father. She gave Dominic a bag of stones. Her gifts were always educational; you should know. Isla was the one that thought you had skill with a switchblade. She gave you your first set of daggers, don't you remember? For me it was speed, hence the jacks made of uncut gems. I left that bag in a police precinct in Shadow Bay, Maryland. It's now housed in the Federal Building in that very same town."

CHAPTER 43

When they reached the states, Phaedra pulled Val from Alana's grasp. Some of the same doctors and nurses who'd taken care of Alana descended on Val, starting IVs, and putting her on a heart monitor. Phaedra hovered near Val's head, pressing kisses to her forehead and whispering something in her ear.

Val's gaze never left Alana's face.

"Take her back to the hotel. If she resists, kill her." Phaedra flipped her blonde braids back over her shoulders."

"I won't resist, Phaedra. In a few hours you'll have your precious stone and then we can finally end this."

Ignoring her, Phaedra continued to murmur something in Val's ear. As the door to the ambulance closed, Alana saw Phaedra pick up the stone that dangled from the chain around Val's neck. Her face shriveled in disgust as she studied it. Val reached up and grabbed the stone from her hand and tucked it down in her shirt.

Cass watched his guard start to nod off while watching television. As much as he tried to focus on the last few weeks of captivity and being carted from one place to another, his thoughts kept returning to the last time he'd seen Alana.

"Give these rings to someone that deserves them. You're free now, Cassiel." Her words echoed in the recesses of his soul. Their union, no matter how brief, was Alana's way of saying goodbye. In the vault and even in his hotel her sweet body yielded to him, nourished him. But it was there in her kiss and the feel of her love, sweet and wet against his skin. She wanted him. Alana, the silent woman standing by his side, who seemed to need nothing and no one, needed him…wanted him.

Can I have you, Cassiel?

He closed his eyes against the waves of emotion careening through him.

Twins, he thought. Alana was carrying his twins and even as she told him, Cass knew he hadn't been fair. Her steely logic hadn't dulled over the years. Her periscope still ran much higher than his. To get her home, he had to trust her. Not Val, not Phaedra, but the woman that danced with him in the quiet of their bedroom. The woman who, in the middle of a blood feud, managed to comfort him.

Cass blinked back tears while he waited for the man to be in a deep sleep before rising from his chair near the window. At once the man was awake and aiming his gun at him.

"Easy, I'm just going to the little boy's room." He pointed in the direction of the bathroom, and the man got up to follow him. No sooner had they reached the bathroom door than Cass turned on the man, and they started wrestling over the gun.

Upon entering the hotel, Alana heard the distant sound of two shots being fired.

* * *

Mark watched as Monet and Gabriel sat on the sofa in the living room staring out the window. Myra came to stand beside him.

"Baby, I don't think they can take much more of this. We haven't heard from Cass for weeks. Levine's not taking any calls. I got turned away from the office an hour ago. These children need their parents. I mean, yeah, we can stand in as Godparents, but nobody can raise them like Cass and Alana."

"Alana knew what she was doing when she trained her children. Cass knew what he was doing when he married Alana. We must trust them. It's all we have." Myra pressed a kiss into his shoulder as she made her way into the living room to the children. "I'm going to see if I can get either one of them to eat something."

Mark's phone buzzed in his pants pocket, and he walked into the kitchen to answer it. He saw Cass's number on the caller ID and quickly moved outside.

"Where the merry fuck have you been?" Mark whispered harshly as he stepped out onto the back porch.

"Good to hear from you, too, Mark. How are my children?"

"How the fuck do you think they are? Where's Alana?"

"I'm at the Federal Building. Can you get here?"

"I'm already in the car."

CHAPTER 44

Cass leaned against the window in Levine's office. He watched the last rays of sunlight leaving a patchwork of color that reminded him of the crochet blanket Alana was working on. He tried to take in a deep breath that stopped short of its purpose.

"I just can't wrap my mind around it, Cass. All of this over some stones?"

Cass glanced up at Levine's reflection in the window and turned. "Splinter of Heaven has been fought over since before Alana was even born. Generations waged war over a stone that started off the size of a rolling pin and was subsequently cut into three pieces. Each piece alone could buy a small country. For all I know, maybe it did."

"And you're telling me that it was Alana's birthright?"

Cass winced at the sound of her name. It was hard not to think of her pulling his rings from her hand.

"Give these to someone that deserves them." Alana's words clawed his gut. He wanted to be angry with her. Needed to be angry with her,

but again her logic had surpassed his. As much as he hated to admit it, Val had been right. Alana walking away from him that night had saved his life.

"Isla was more than a common jewel thief. She was Alana's mother. Isla was royalty. Whether she shunned her throne or lost it in a coup doesn't matter now. Isla brought this stone across the desert so she could take care of her children, but it brought her nothing but heartache. Just as it's done for pretty much everyone that's ever touched the damned thing. You once called those legal pads that Alana wrote her statement on "The Holy Grail", and it was. What we didn't know was that it was also the key that tied together so many things, including Julian Barlow's fascination with Alana. He knew about the stones and her parentage. He was willing to cast aside all those girls that were in his stable, including Phaedra Khalid, not for Alana, but for those stones. Dominic Mandylor was his brother and attorney, but he specialized in real estate and in diamond brokerages and acquisitions."

Cass took his seat once more and looked at Levine. "In the beginning I figured, that maybe once Phaedra got the stones it would be over. Then I talked to Val, and I realized that as much as it was about the stone, it really wasn't. This was about settling a score."

Levine shook his head in confusion. Just then, one of his men came to the door, and Levine waved him in.

Mark barged past him. "Cass, man where the fuck have you been? You dropped off the map. Nobody could find you. And this one here wasn't giving up any information.

"There was nothing to tell, Mark. We couldn't find him either."

Mark flopped down in the chair next to Cass. "You look like shit, Cass. Scratch that. You look like fried shit."

"My kids okay?" Cass asked tiredly.

"You already know they're not. Myra's got her hands full with them. Hasn't let them out of her sight since you left. Took them both to work at the center to keep their minds occupied. Where's Alana? She with you?"

Cass took in a breath that made his chest hitch with unshed tears. He shook his head.

"She's not dead, Mark, but she's barely hanging on."

"Thought you said she wasn't hurt, Cass," Levine said quietly.

"Her wounds are healing on the inside, but I know my wife. Julian Barlow thought she was a machine and almost ran her in the ground. Phaedra Khalid is no different. Like I said, I thought it was about a stone. Maybe in the beginning it was. Phaedra is as greedy as Julian."

Cass's dark gaze searched Levine's desk surface for a long moment before he felt Mark's hand come to rest on his arm. "Val—Valerie Banks—has been the buffer between Phaedra and Alana. She stitched up Monet and has been taking care of Alana since..."

"Cass, you said something about settling an old score," Levine offered.

"I don't understand. Cass, how did you manage to get away? They had you locked up, isn't that why you didn't call?"

Cass smiled sadly. "Wasn't hard. Just like before, I was the incentive to keep my wife's head down and her hands busy, but I wasn't Phaedra's primary concern. She wanted to punish—wants to punish—Alana for what she thinks was stolen from her both times. Julian and now Val."

"Val? But Alana's not gay."

"No, she's not. Alana's motives are simpler than that." Cass looked over at Mark. "Val was one of Alana's children,."

"I don't understand. Cass, what does this have to do with...?"

Cass waved his hand to silence Mark. He looked over at Levine. "Only three people other than Alana know what ever happened to that bag of jacks Alana used to play with."

"You mean the one with millions of dollars' worth of uncut gemstones? The one she dropped on that desk at the precinct?" Mark asked.

Cass nodded slowly. But his gaze never left Levine's face as the stark realization filled the man's eyes. "She poured the stones into my hands once. All shapes, sizes, and colors. Alana told me that Dominic brought her to Isla and Knox for training. She told me that Dominic's gifts were always educational. I heard some of the men talking, and apparently one of them drove Alana and Val to a refinery in Mogadishu. He spoke of a bag loaded with gemstones. I only know of one that Alana had."

"That's impossible, Cass. We have facial recognition software on every camera in this building."

Cass sighed as he felt Alana move through his blood, quickening the bond between them so sharply that he quaked inside.

"The stone would be about the size of a golf ball, roughly hewn and unrefined. Probably to cover the value because if anyone shined that thing up…. Teacher knew who and what Alana was, and he carried it to the grave. He and Harvey Knox were friends and partners. He knew what Isla had put in the bag of jacks."

"Alana can't be in this building, Cass. This place is a fortress. State of the Art surveillance equipment... Pentagon strength shit."

"Then you really don't know my wife, do you, Levine? It was one of the special projects Teacher put Alana on. We all remember how they liked to use my wife's particular talent for getting into impossible places."

Levine grabbed the phone, and just as he moved to punch in a number, alarms sounded in the building and red and blue lights began to flash.

* * *

Val looked up at Alana as she poured the gemstones into Val's hands. The stones clicked and clacked like old bones. Val slid to her knees as if the stones were suddenly too heavy to hold. There, sitting amidst the rubies, sapphires, uncultured pearls, and a green super ball sat the last remnant of the Splinter of Heaven.

"You're in the clear, Alana." Val said plucking the stone from one hand and holing up to the light.

"What are you talking about?"

"By all rights, I have the stone. It's my face on the cameras. They can't pin it to you."

"Cass knows. He's not a stupid man. He may have pieced it all together."

"Doesn't matter. My face is the only one they saw. Why do you think I had you dress in that suit? Brian brought the prototype to me a few years ago."

"How'd you get in, Val? I built the system. I knew the weaknesses."

"You said it yourself. You weren't the only one Isla and Knox trained."

Alana shook out the bag, and Val poured the jewels back into it. Alana cinched the bag shut and handed it to her.

"Teacher couldn't wrap his mind around why. I mean there was only enough bail money to pay your bail ten times over. Just enough for ten girls. Only ten. Phaedra was already taken care of, even after she had me and a couple of her friends beat you up so badly. You took care of her anyway. She could leave with the rest of the girls, did leave. Nobody knew about the last girl, the one that got picked up for boosting a car to go get her brother from her father's house. No one knew I was there in that cell, except you. You gave up the tenth spot…"

"Shh, Val. Don't talk anymore."

"You wanna know why she hates you? Phaedra hates you because after everything she did to you, you paid for her freedom anyway, gave up your place in line to pay for mine, for us. No gift she gave me was greater than that. She couldn't compete. I gave her my name, but you.... It would always be you, Alana. "

The tears flowed over the hollows in Val's cheeks. Alana reached out to smooth away the tears, and the vault doors blew open. Val opened her coat to put the bag inside as the federal agents swarmed in. She reached behind her back and pulled both of her guns. Suddenly the air was filled with the sound of gunfire.

"Wait!" Cass roared. "That's my family in there!"

Alana turned to see Val staring at the small hole in the front of her coat. Val staggered back and slid down the wall leaving a cruel smear of blood as she sat down hard on the floor. She opened her coat to see the blood stain spreading slowly across her side. Alana came went to her and fell to her knees. Alana tore her sleeve from her shirt and pressed it against Val's side.

Val gripped weakly at Alana's wrist. "Get away… get out of here."

"I won't leave you here, Val." Alana shook her head softly as tears spilled over her cheeks.

Val reached up and touched Alana's face leaving a smear of blood.

"You made me leave you in that precinct back in Robey, Alana. I know what they did to you. Should have been me"

Alana hugged her tighter

"Shouldn't have happen to anyone, Val."

Val reached up and cupped Alana's cheek.

"You made me leave. You paid for my freedom."

"Shh, it doesn't matter." Alana kissed the palm of Val's hand as she tried to keep pressure on the wound.

"Course it matters. *You* always mattered." A thick runnel of blood spilled from the corner of Val's mouth'

"I won't leave you. I won't, Val, I won't." Alana pulled Val onto her lap and began to rock her slowly back and forth.

"You made a way for us...for me. My turn now. My plans never changed." Val clutched the bag of stones to her flattened chest as she turned her face into Alana's arm and breathed her in. "Tell Cass he was right about me. Married Phaedra... loved you."

Val took in another breath, and then she went still.

CHAPTER 45

Cass stood in the observation room watching Alana sit with her back pressed to the wall in the far corner of the room. Her bloody clothes had been replaced with a sweatsuit and a pair of socks, both three sizes too big. The hollowness in her voice made him fill up more than once as she gave her statement. Never once did she ask for him. Never once did she look up at the mirror.

"I just got word, Cass. Alana won't be charged with anything." Levine bustled into the room and sat on the table

He turned and looked at Levine. "But you said..."

"No fingerprints or DNA other than Valerie Banks's. Her face is all over the facial recognition software. She is the one that tripped the alarms. She looked dead into the camera quite a few times."

"Alana was in the vault, stands to reason. You said there would be no golden parachutes this time. Alana won't survive being in prison again. My kids won't survive it. She'll carry our babies to term, but she won't come back to me. She told me she would never take our kids from me, but she never said she would stay." Cass's voice broke and he looked back through the glass.

"One last gift from Harvey Knox and Isla—and Teacher—and yeah, maybe even Valerie Banks. That bug, you know the one with the legs and lots of progeny? Let me tell you, those progenies are lethal. Val left a business ledger with Brian and told him if she died what he should do with it. Take Alana home, Cass. Love her a lot." Levine patted Cass on his shoulder before he left the room.

* * *

Alana watched as the agent walked out of the room before wrapping her arms around her midsection, huddling even closer to the wall and turning to face it. The last time she'd seen Cass, he'd drawn her back against his chest as Val's body was gathered into a body bag.

She could feel him watching her through the observation glass in the interrogation room. She took in a breath that made her chest ache as she heard the door to the integration room open once more. She didn't even bother to turn around when his warm, manly scent surrounded her. She felt Cass's hand come to rest on her back causing her skin to tingle.

"Alana…" he managed, his voice wrought with emotion, "you said something about not deserving my rings. Well, let me tell you, it's me that doesn't deserve you. I don't. I've hurt you in so many ways. I was wrong, and I'm sorry. I don't deserve you, but I am asking…please come home to me. You asked for forever once. Now it's my turn."

Alana threw herself into his arms.

CHAPTER 46

Three weeks later...

Alana watched Gabriel's bus turn the corner. Monet was back at school, and Cass had gone to pick up some bagels for breakfast. Alana settled into her rocking chair and slowly began to rock. She ran her hand over the soft swell of the babies she was carrying.

In the background, the newscaster was rambling on about the weather and traffic reports before tossing the newsfeed back to a news anchor that Alana hated.

She knew for a fact that the man was into boys and that he enjoyed cruising the strip where Alana found most, if not all, the children that resided at her center. She smiled and picked up her crochet project and worked another row knowing full well that the Sex Crimes Department of the Shadow Bay PD was about to make a visit to the news station courtesy of an anonymous tip and some photographs.

"And in local news, a fire in the slaughterhouse district destroyed three abandoned buildings. There were no casualties, but the arson investigators found what looked like a bouldering wall in one of the buildings. No injuries were reported."

Alana continued to rock. The beds were made, and she planned to make spaghetti that evening. The ground beef was already thawing on the counter. She could hear the soft chime of the washing machine signaling that the load of towels was finished and waiting for the dryer.

She looked over at the vase of blue lilies that had arrived the other day. The card never held a name, but Val's left-handed scrawl was always there. Sometimes the card read, 'Today and tomorrow'. Other cards read 'Now and forever'.

Alana looked down at the remnants of the burnt card next to her mug. She could barely make out the swirling cursive E in the word Eternity. Val was the only one that knew when her true birthday was, and for as long as Alana could remember the flowers found their way to her every year on her birthday or a few weeks later.

"A body was found in a local cemetery. Police say the body of former FBI agent Brian Mitchell was found on what appears to be the grave of his father with a self-inflicted gunshot wound to the head. Investigators are saying that the agent was under investigation for corruption and various other charges. Coming up, more live coverage from Cybex Women's Detention Center where reputed drug queen pin, Phaedra Khalid, and several other women walked away from their work release site. Officials say that the bodies of two prisoners were found on the premises, and at least three others were apprehended a short distance from the all-female facility which is the counterpart to the all-male facility out in Jessup. No word on the apprehension of Khalid, but she is considered armed and dangerous."

Alana slid to the floor as she pulled out the bag of uncut gems and cast them on the floor in front of her. Alana heard the creak on the steps long before she saw Phaedra's reflection in the bay window. Alana sighed before she tossed the green super ball in the air and began to pick up the pieces. "Hello, Phaedra, I've been waiting for you."

"Had me in the fields working like a fucking slave. They made me cut my hair and my nails. Held me down like an animal. You did this... you brought me to this."

Alana studied Phaedra's reflection for a long moment. The lace-front wig Phaedra wore was matted in places, and it hung in greasy ringlets around her acne scarred face. Only one of her bluer than blue contact lenses remained. Phaedra's other eye stared out from smears of mascara. The rage, the madness Alana saw there made Phaedra's dark brown eye seem even darker.

"You took everything from me."

Phaedra raised the knife Alana had noticed was missing from the dish drain that morning. She watched as the unmistakable glimmer of an infrared laser sight cut through the morning air, followed by a single shot the pierced the front window.

Alana never turned when she heard Phaedra crumple to the floor. She simply tossed the ball in the air once more, but this time she missed and watched the ball bounce across the floor. She ran her hand over her unborn children as she pushed herself to her feet and walked over to the front door. The red and blue lights of the police units washed over her, and she walked into Cass' arms.

STEPHANIE M FREEMAN is a Hybrid author that began her professional writing career back in 2012 when Crimson Romance, an imprint of Simon & Schuster published her novel, *Necessary Evil.* Since then, she has explored different writing genres including, Mysteries, Thrillers, Romantic Suspense and the Paranormal. Stephanie is also a member of Naleighna Kai's Tribe Called Success and the Cavalcade of Authors. She often jokes that with a shot glass or a cup of coffee in one hand, she is known for writing an erotic tale or two. Stephanie has amassed a loyal group of fans who eagerly await her latest releases. Her Diamonds, Blood and Shadows Series is a fan favorite. Her other books include Unfinished Business, Nature of the Beast and A Letter from Yesay. Writing as Aracyne (Air Ruh Sin) Kelly, she also wrote: Peculiar Kindness and Heaven's Girl.

Stephanie is the host of the wildly popular Club House Event called Murder, Mayhem and Mysteries (and the people who love them). With multiple five-star reviews of her work, Stephanie M. Freeman continues to push literary boundaries.

Visit Stephanie on the Web:
www.stephaniemfreemanauthor.com

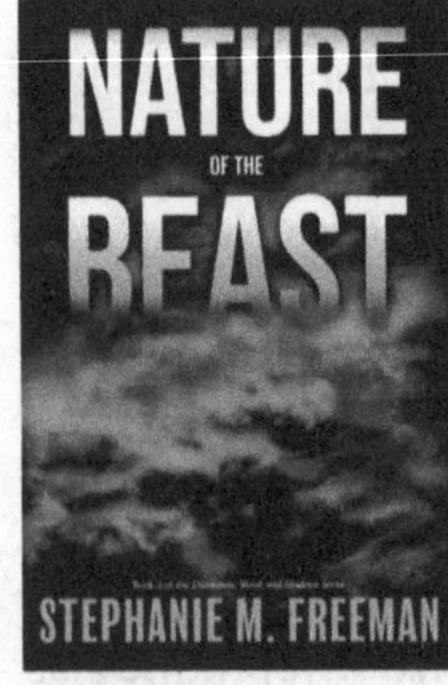

Nature of the Beast: Book Three in the Diamonds Blood and Shadows Series

Hush now; you're dying. The golden hour has come and gone. With the extent of your injuries the recovery would be a slow and painful process. But you're in luck. Mercy is my stock and trade.

Now now, we both know that licking your lips to lubricate the lie was the first mistake. And please, excuses are little more than truth turned inside out. So many apologies but they all go against the grain.

May I join you? Not in dying silly. That's your job, now. The previous one I gave you well… Can I be frank? My name is Kevin Francis Greer but, in discussions like these honesty and nicknames go hand in hand.

You think me a monster and you're right. Wasn't always like this. When I was ten, Mama held my foot to a hotplate for some real or imagined slight. Papa watched from his grey recliner in the living room inhaling the acrid smoke from the cigar he lit with a match.

Wooden ones were best as the tobacco burned evenly. Lighters are infinitely more personal. Hold one under a person's nose and it will light like the wick of a candle and burn forever burn until there's nothing left that looks human, but then you know that now, don't you? Don't you? Yes, I think you do.

This whole dirty business was nothing like the red coil feasting on my heel at the time. The hot plate with its lone eye worked as desired if not as designed. The orgasm that leapt from me left quite the mess on the maroon shag carpet. Mama's disgust became my inspiration. Papa's pride became my muse. Music like pain is an acquired taste, unique to each person. Your short shallow breaths remind me of a young Vivaldi or an older Beethoven. Both were poets for the dead as am I.

The assignment was simple Endicott. Follow Willow Daniels. Make yourself indispensable to her. Protect her at all costs. The MacGuffin beneath her skin is more valuable than gold or flames. Lost in the folds of her mind is an answer to a question I asked forty years ago.

Nearly killed her when I asked in person. My passion got the better of me, I'll admit, but pain makes a captive audience of us all. Nothing seemed to work on the boy with her, though. Peppering him with questions after each slice did nothing but solidify his resolve to remain silent. Sirens wailing in the distance cut my interview and their date night short.

My ex-wife was neat in her grave, nigh ten years. Such a cunning little beast she was. Hiding our son. Adopting him out was a stroke of genius. Hot plates and cigars were not part of his future. Short money filled my bolt holes and bank accounts to the brim. He would have been a God among insects. So much to tell him. So much to share. A dream deferred to be sure.

You failed so horribly. But then, thinking is a chore for mammals like you. Romance was not in the job description. It's why the scent of your aftershave was replaced by the fragrance of soot and burning flesh. Of course, I'll dab away the tear spilling from the remains of your eye. As I stated earlier, mercy is my stock and trade.

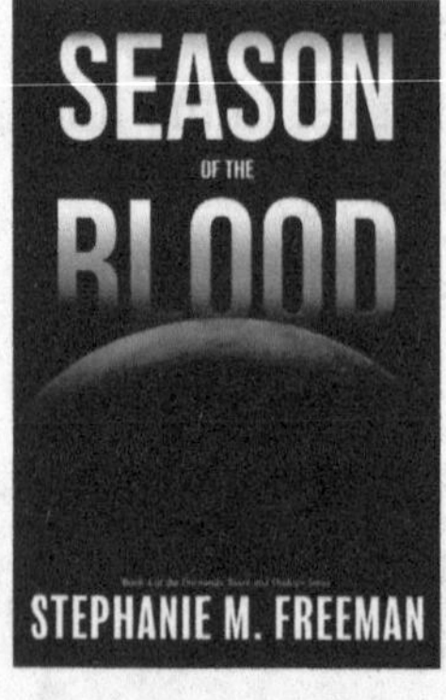

Book Excerpt from Season of the Blood: Book Four in the Shadows, Blood and Diamonds Series

I am not one or the other.

Names are petty and mine never fit no how. It's enough that I exist. Profound and profane is good enough for me. I am perfect in my otherness, believe that.

I *am* something else.

Such a simple truth that dogged my steps from the time I was born. Can't say my parents loved me, you understand. On the outside I resembled every little girl all decked out in barrettes and bows. Under my skirts… well that was another story entirely. Never thought anything was right or wrong with me until the games started with Daddy.

I won't bore you with the particulars. Spare me the tears and the guilt that passes for sympathy. All you need to know is that by my twelfth birthday Daddy was in the ground and I put him there. Planted him better than any undertaker or gardener. You don't get to know how I finished him neither.

All you need to know is that he died screaming. Made damned sure of that. I even joined him at one point… in screaming that is. Laughed a little too.

Mamma married again and you'd think she'd trade up. Hearing the grunts and groans and the occasional gag before she bolted to the bathroom served as a marker. What she couldn't abide, and more or less let slide I was assigned to.

To keep the peace…. Hell, maybe to take her place on account of the new baby on the way. Out with the old and in with the new, I guess. Hoped it wasn't true. Prayed it wasn't, but then I heard the floor creak and my doorknob turn. You know how the story goes.

Can't stay anywhere for free.

Frying pan to the fire. Rolled out with the clothes on my back and a sweaty, crumpled five in my pocket. Won't tell you how I earned that or about my first night's peace. You see my otherness had its perks and buyers. Some meaner than others, but it was business; nothing personal.

Snuffling back blood and spitting out a tooth or two makes you humble or mean. I chose the latter and had a good run until I didn't. That was where she found me. Hair like flames; green eyes like hellfire. Never said a word. Just sat there in an alley that reeked of piss, vomit, and my own fear. Sat there as fine as you please on a wooden milk crate next to the pile of garbage I'd been thrown in.

Followed her I don't remember how many city blocks. Thought I lost her in the shadows of the streetlights. It was almost daylight before we got to where she was going. She unlocked the door to an apartment and went in leaving the choice to me.

It is one I will never regret.

It's why I'm here with grey eyes, sagging breasts and a silver beard to match. Filed my teeth down to points and forked my tongue. Can lick many things in many directions and I often do. People think me a monster, and I am. I live, lie, and fuck all in equal measure.

Male…female or something else on the menu, I don't discriminate. I run it all; buy and sell it all. It's what I am, who I am and what I do.

And I'm good at it.

With a shot glass in one hand and a blunt dangling from the corner of my mouth I am the one your Mamma couldn't conjure in her worse night terror. But to her…. Not Mamma, you dumb shit. The one that saved my life and straightened my crown of bones.

To her I am Blood. I'd kill or die for her.

And that's even after I betrayed her.

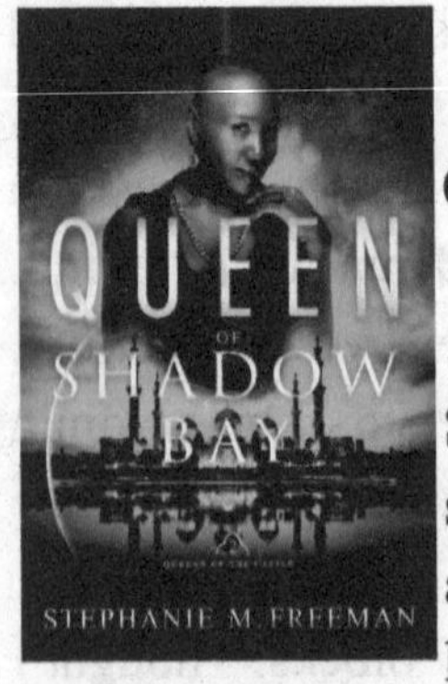

Queen of Shadow Bay- Book Two in the Queens of the Castle Series

Smothering his wife was easier than watching her sleep. The bovine, simpering way she scampered after him was cute in the beginning. Her serving him hand and foot even tickled his dick once. Just. Once. Now her 'Yes, Baby. Whatever you say Honey Man' made his skin crawl.

Gerald Newland sat his keys in the small wooden bowl his wife lovingly placed on the table near the staircase. The gorge burning the back of his throat intensified at the prospect of lying down next to his dearly beloved. He'd perfected the skill of not flinching when she touched him, but even that was beginning to fray. He glanced at their wedding portrait on the wall and admired the smug look on his face.

Carpathia "Carrie" Newland stood before a church filled with all her rotting menopausal friends wearing a cream-colored pants suit and a colorful scarf that reminded him of cheap stained glass. The bouquet she carried was little more than a Styrofoam ball with a stick shoved up its ass. The hand crocheted pink and white flowers stuck to it matched the one in her platinum grey wig with the baby hair combed into place. What old prune had baby hair? Most of that shit ran to the back of their heads by the time they hit fifty.

Why the old bitties insisted on telling her she looked like an angel was beyond him. Anyone with beer goggles could tell the woman was no prize.

"A little make up or paint makes even an ugly one what she ain't." He whispered before kicking off his shoes and heading upstairs.

But that stock portfolio *mmmm hmmm*, that thing alone put all the pretty little bitches to shame. The old girl was smart with her money and that was a plus. What Gerald couldn't run through the damn sure intended to spend on anything and anyone that pleased him including his stepdaughter Pamela from his first marriage or was it the third.

He'd lost count over the years.

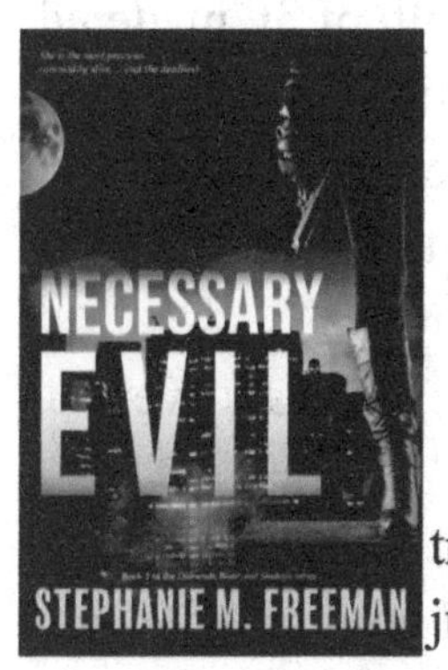

Necessary Evil

Chapter 1

Apologies were petty in her line of work. Gaining trust and turning it against the unsuspecting wasn't just easy, it was pathetic. The bovine look of horror made her laugh when she was younger. Now, it just hurt. Maggie Ludlow's costume consisted of a cream-colored blouse and a black pencil skirt and modest heels. The wire rimmed glasses she tossed on the desk were as real as the objective. Soundless was best, but bloodless was better.

"Stupid." She hissed.

"Rough day?" The deep whiskey smooth voice washed down on her.

His eyes were the same: dark, fathomless. Whispers of the boy she remembered haunted the corners of his features. The gun and detective's shield were new, as was the bullet proof vest he wore. Maggie eyed the name tag on his chest, and bit down on a curse.

Not now, please God. Not now.

She cleared her throat and smoothed a hand over the blouse and skirt. Poise and grace were tools just like the gun strapped to his hip.

"Excuse me Officer…." Maggie slipped on her glasses before pushing a fine wisp of hair that fell from her chignon back into place.

"Sergeant Cassiel Garrett, Homicide." He corrected, as he stuck out his hand. "Is Mrs. Shaw in by any chance?"

Maggie chewed on her bottom lip as her gut sank further south. There was no mention of a sister in the dossier.

Great. This has to be one of Julian's really bad jokes, or did someone forget to check the backgrounds of the bank manager and her employees?

How could her true employer, crime lord Julian Barlow expect her to effectively rob a bank or complete any of the heists assigned to her and the crew without the information she requested? Floorplans… staffing… surveillance cameras…alarm systems and exits; all of it mattered. Success depended on those crucial bits of information. Without them the 'No blood, no sound' rule fell flat, and people died.

Maggie studied the detective's scarred hand as it hovered between them.

There was no mention in the dossier about a sister, but years overseas training meant years out of contact.

"Yeah, it's pretty ugly huh?" Cass turned his hand as if to study it.

Maggie continued to stare past the burn scars and mull over the new variable standing before her.

I even asked why the information on the manager was so limited. There had to be more. His mother could have easily remarried or had another child. Fostering children wasn't out of the realm.

Julian had to be playing with her. Sometimes he did it just to see her improvise. The deaths of innocent bystanders were Julian's kind of entertainment, but they never factored into her equation. Maggie made sure of it. Information was power and Julian had effectively cut her off at the knees

"You know what? It's ok. You don't have to shake my hand." He flexed his hand slightly as if offended by the raised scar on the back of it.

Maggie blinked suddenly remembering that he was there. When Detective Sergeant Garrett moved to lower his hand, she extended hers.

"Not all heroes wear medals." Maggie shook his hand once and backed away.

"Thanks, I never saw myself as a…" a flash of humor crossed his face.

"Mrs. Shaw is on a conference call." Maggie interrupted turning in the general direction of her manager's door. "I can show you in if you..."

Maggie's gut spun into a cruel knot. In the time it took to look at the door, the detective was beside her resting his hand on hers. She hazarded another glance at the crazy quilt of agony that marred his semi-sweet chocolate hand.

Pulling away was not an option. Such things were frowned upon and easily led to trips to the emergency room. Maggie willed herself to look into his eyes once more. His smile seemed genuine enough, but even they could be faked. Maggie knew all too well what lurked beneath the smiles of men.

"Lydia, I mean Mrs. Shaw, is my sister. I can show myself in." he moved to leave then thought better of it. "Hey, listen, I'm sorry I scared you."

Maggie nodded once and waited for him to release her hand. His presence, like a shadow, receded as he made his way back to the office. Once the door was closed, Maggie spilled into her chair.

The sister would be bad enough if she didn't stay in her office, but the brother would have been worse.

Great, another death on my conscience.

* * *

Cass stood near the door inside his sister's office watching her searching four monitors stationed at varying heights on the desk.

"You used to have that same look on your face when you did your homework." He grinned as he leaned against the door.

"Well don't you look all armed and dangerous." Lydia peered at him over her glasses and smiled. How'd you manage to get past the front desk like that?" she asked pulling off her bifocals and tossing them on the large calendar resting under her keyboard.

"Harvey was out back taking his usual smoke break." Cass pointed with his thumb. "Think I scared your receptionist though." A sheepish grin tipped the corners of his mouth. "Then again you do look fearsome behind that desk. Cracking the whip, I see."

"Maggie Ludlow's a temp, but she's world's better than the last one. Timid but good. We're thinking about hiring her on permanently." Lydia rolled her eyes before scribbling a signature on a form and tossing it on a stack of papers. I'm beginning to think there's more paperwork in this place then money."

Cass looked back in the direction of the door before settling down in the chair. A wry smile spread over his face. Lydia sat back and folded her arms.

"What?" he smiled harder as her eyebrows made their little vee of annoyance.

"You know what. You and your special dark chocolate skin and that 'drop the drawers' smooth voice of yours. Do you ever go anywhere and not have droves of women falling all over you?"

He grinned and cast another look over his shoulder.

"Apparently not everyone is blinded by my shocking good looks. Maggie the Temp took one look at my hands and said something strange—Not all heroes wear medals." In truth her statement flattered him, but the look on her face left Cass unsettled.

"Maggie frightens easily. I'm surprised she didn't wilt at the sight of you in all that gear." Her gaze dropped to his hand as she frowned. "She's right. Not all heroes wear medals. Some wear scars."

Cass thought of the woman at the front desk. Maggie looked vulnerable, yes but not fainthearted. She didn't even pull away in disgust like other women did at the sight of his hands. Instead her emerald gaze drifted over the scars as if familiar maybe not with the pattern, but the source.

He'd only wanted to comfort her when he put his hand on hers, but then her countenance changed. She didn't wince but the color drained from her face. He wasn't one prone to apologizing without cause but the idea of her being afraid of him poked at a raw place inside.

Cass made a mental note to check the lobby and the surroundings out on his way back to his car. Benjamin Greer in Robbery would be his first stop once he got back to the precinct. A look at the robbery reports would give him an even better perspective on any trouble in the area.

Lydia scooted up to her desk and stacked her hands on the calendar as her face clouded with grief. The memory of her screaming at the sight of him at the burn unit all those years ago still haunted him.

"Maggie The Temp seeing anybody?" Cass raised his voice just enough to gain her attention while busying a hand with extracting the cell phone from a pocket.

"Wait a minute. First you say you scared the girl, now you want her number. What about Tracy, your girlfriend?" she tilted her head slightly. "You remember her, don't you?"

"We're done. Her cat Jasper hid when she came back for the rest of her things."

Cass watched as she latched onto the distraction. Anything had to be better than watching Lydia's face fill with sadness every time she looked at his hands. Didn't matter how well his hands functioned. The scars put his sister and everyone else on edge. He glanced over his shoulder and smiled.

"Maggie The Temp have a last name? She married? Got any kids?" his smile brought an immediate mischief to the conversation.

Lydia threw a wad of paper at him.

"Okay, okay, I get the message." Cass easily plucked the paper from the air and pitched it into the wastepaper basket sitting against the far wall behind her desk.

"So, what are you doing here? Besides checking out my secretary's ass?"

"I just came to say hi and to tell you I can't make it for dinner."

"You cancelled last week." The frown of disappointment deepened the wrinkle between her eyebrows.

"I'm in the middle of an investigation, Lyddy." His expression was one of complete unconcern. The mere mention of his job as a homicide detective was usually enough to quell the need for excuses.

"You're always in the middle of some big case. You do have a life and family beyond that badge you know." Lydia nodded in the direction of the detective's shield hanging from the chain around his neck.

Just then the phone rang, Cass rolled his eyes and thumbed through his phone. Lydia snatched the receiver from the desk phone and put it to her ear. He watched as her mouth fell open. Lydia turned to look at one of the screens. Cass stood and looked at one of the monitors. The red lights flashing for the silent alarm flickered on the control panel on her desk

"But everything looks normal. I don't understand." She tapped a button on the laptop to switch to another view of the bank lobby. Everything looked normal.

Cass reached over and pressed the speaker button on the telephone. The rapid buck of gunfire cut people off mid scream.

* * *

Leaving her post wasn't an option. Staying in the back was an even bigger mistake. Collateral damage was all that was left. The deaths in the lobby were regrettable. It was all about damage control, now. The extraction team was rolling, and it was all about saving the ones she could. The threat was always there but eliminating it; lowering the number of casualties was priority number one.

"Fall back." Maggie tapped the earpiece. The transmitter in her left crackled to life. "Leap frog it. Evasive maneuvers now!" She whispered. "Get to the extraction point." Maggie said louder as she rose from the desk while casting a look back over her shoulder.

One scream became many. Rapid fire crowded the air, cutting off a voice calling for God. Maggie heard her manager's door open as footsteps thundered down the hall in front of her. The team she worked with had their instructions. Killing was the last resort. She cast a look over her shoulder. The detective was running toward her with his gun drawn.

Maggie sidestepped his grip and rounded the desk.

"Maggie, get behind me!" he yelled. "Maggie stop!"

She's just as important as the score. Kill whoever you have to but get her out of there. Julian's last instruction to the group filled her mind.

Making it to the door was the only option now. Maybe they'd grab her and go before the cop crossed the last three feet to the door.

"Maggie stop." The detective's hand scrabbled across her shoulder as a series of sharp loud pops of gunfire filled the air.

And then, the world went black.

Synopsis:

On the Dark Web, Alanna Symone is the most precious commodity alive. Fathoms below in Deep Web, she is also the deadliest. Can hard-nosed, Homicide Detective Cassiel Garrett, figure out her next move or will a "Necessary Evil" kill them both?

www.ingramcontent.com/pod-product-compliance
Lightning Source LLC
Chambersburg PA
CBHW012014050726
47590CB00009B/3179